D1126151

THE BASKETBALL GAME

Warning: This book, which is based on a true story, has depictions of anti-Semitism and contains racial stereotypes and hateful language. It is intended for an audience of 12 years and older.

National Film Board of Canada Collection

THE
BASKETBALL GAME

A GRAPHIC NOVEL

WRITTEN BY

HART SNIDER

ART BY

SEAN COVERNTON

FIREFLY BOOKS

A FIREFLY BOOK

Published under license. Copyright © 2022 National Film Board of Canada
Book design and adaptation copyright © 2022 Firefly Books Ltd.
Text copyright © 2022 Hart Snider
Photographs on page 87 copyright © as listed below

Adapted from The Basketball Game © 2011 National Film Board of Canada

First printing

Library of Congress Control Number: 2022934049

Library and Archives Canada Cataloguing in Publication
Title: The basketball game : a graphic novel / written by Hart Snider ; art by Sean Covernton.
Names: Snider, Hart, author. | Covernton, Sean, artist.
Series: National Film Board of Canada collection.
Description: Series statement: National Film Board of Canada collection | Adapted from the animated short film The basketball game (2011, National Film Board of Canada).
Identifiers: Canadiana 20220189390 | ISBN 9780228103912 (hardcover)
Subjects: LCGFT: Comics adaptations. | LCGFT: Comics (Graphic works)
Classification: LCC PN6733.S65 B37 2022 | DDC 741.5/971—dc23

Published in the United States by
Firefly Books (U.S.) Inc.
P.O. Box 1338, Ellicott Station
Buffalo, New York 14205

Published in Canada by
Firefly Books Ltd.
50 Staples Avenue, Unit 1
Richmond Hill, Ontario L4B 0A7

Cover design: National Film Board of Canada and Hartley Millson
Interior design: Hart Snider and Sam Tse
Coloration and adaptations to basketball game sequence: Sam Tse

Page 20 (top panel): Source photo of the Jewish Community Centre courtesy of JAHSENA
Photo credits for page 87:
Top left: Photo provided by Hart Snider
Top right: Howie Silverman
Middle left: Wes Machnikowski
Bottom right: Wes Machnikowski

Printed in China

 We acknowledge the financial support of the Government of Canada.

The National Film Board of Canada (NFB) is a leader in exploring animation as an artform, a storytelling medium and innovative content for emerging platforms. It produces trailblazing animated works both in its Montreal studios and across the country, and it works with many of the world's leading creators on international co-productions. NFB productions have won more than 7,000 awards, including seven Oscars for NFB animation and seven grand prizes at the Annecy International Animation Film Festival. To access this unique content, visit NFB.ca.

TO MY PARTNER, COLLABORATOR, INSPIRATION AND BEST FRIEND, GALIT — I LOVE YOU. THANKS FOR ALWAYS BEING RIGHT. THIS BOOK (AND THE FILM IT'S ADAPTING) WOULDN'T EXIST WITHOUT YOU.

TO MY DAUGHTER, LEORA — THANKS FOR REMINDING ME HOW THE WORLD LOOKS FROM A KID'S POINT OF VIEW. I LOVE YOU FOREVER, AND KEEP SHINING BRIGHT.

TO MY PARENTS, RUTH AND EARLE, MY BROTHER, ADAM, AND TO ALL MY FAMILY — THANKS FOR YOUR LOVE, SUPPORT AND INFINITE ENCOURAGEMENT.

— HART SNIDER

HOW DO YOU DEAL WITH FEAR AND PREJUDICE?

That was the challenge faced by Alberta's Jewish community back in the early 1980s, after a parent in Eckville, Alberta, discovered that her son's grade 9 social studies teacher Jim Keegstra was teaching hatred of Jewish people in his classroom. Keegstra's story became big news, and after he was fired there was also a lot of interest in his former students who had been taught so many lies. Did they believe him?

These events happened when I was only nine years old, but I have never forgotten them — not only because of all the bad feelings I had as a Jewish kid growing up in Edmonton who was aware of what was happening not that far away, but also because I was struck by how the parents and the high school principal in Eckville and the leaders in my community approached such an ugly situation by deciding to work together. Outside of the media spotlight, they organized a "day of fun and fellowship" and brought Keegstra's former students to our Jewish summer camp, where they could see for themselves what Jewish people are actually like.

I wanted to share this story, and I first pitched it at a workshop for emerging filmmakers at the National Film Board of Canada, where it was chosen to be produced as a five-minute animated short. In 2011, I collaborated with producer Yves J. Ma, animator Sean Covernton, composer Adam Damelin and executive producer Tracey Friesen, and we spent about six months making the film.

The Basketball Game had its world premiere at a documentary film festival called Global Visions in my hometown of Edmonton, and a few people who were connected to the story were sitting in the audience. One of them told me after the screening that they couldn't believe they were seeing our small community's story being represented in a film, and I still feel exactly the same way.

Also in the audience was an Alberta politician named Janice Sarich (1958–2021), who spoke about the film the next day to the province's Legislative Assembly. She said, "This film is significant, Mr. Speaker, because it is based on the recollections of a nine-year-old boy coming to grips with hate and discrimination in Alberta."

Although a lot has changed since I was a kid, sadly, we are still dealing with many of the same old issues today.

Racism, conspiracy theories and anti-Semitism are spread every day on social media and other platforms. The hate that Keegstra taught in his classroom is now found in memes, videos and forums. Over and over again, we are challenged with the question, how do we deal with fear and prejudice?

I hope we can continue to find common ground and have empathy for each other, but most importantly, I hope that parents and kids keep talking to each other.

We're going to need a lot of basketballs.

Hart Snider
January 1st, 2022

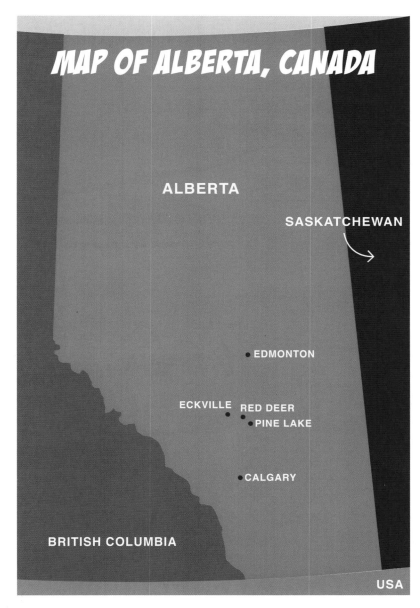

MAP OF ALBERTA, CANADA

ALBERTA

SASKATCHEWAN

• EDMONTON

ECKVILLE **RED DEER**
• • •PINE LAKE

•CALGARY

BRITISH COLUMBIA

USA

This story is set in Pine Lake, Alberta, on Treaty 7 territory — the traditional and ancestral territory of the Blackfoot Confederacy: Kainai, Piikani and Siksika; the Tsuu T'ina Nation; the Stoney Nakoda First Nation, including the Chiniki, Bearspaw and Wesley First Nations; and the Métis Nation of Alberta, Region 3 within the historical Northwest Métis Homeland.

The story also takes place in Edmonton, Alberta, Amiskwaciwâskahikan- ᒥᐢᑿᒌᐤ, on Treaty 6 territory — the traditional and ancestral territory of the Cree, Dene, Blackfoot, Saulteaux and Nakota Sioux, as well as the Métis Settlements and the Métis Nation of Alberta, Regions 2, 3 and 4 within the historical Northwest Métis Homeland.

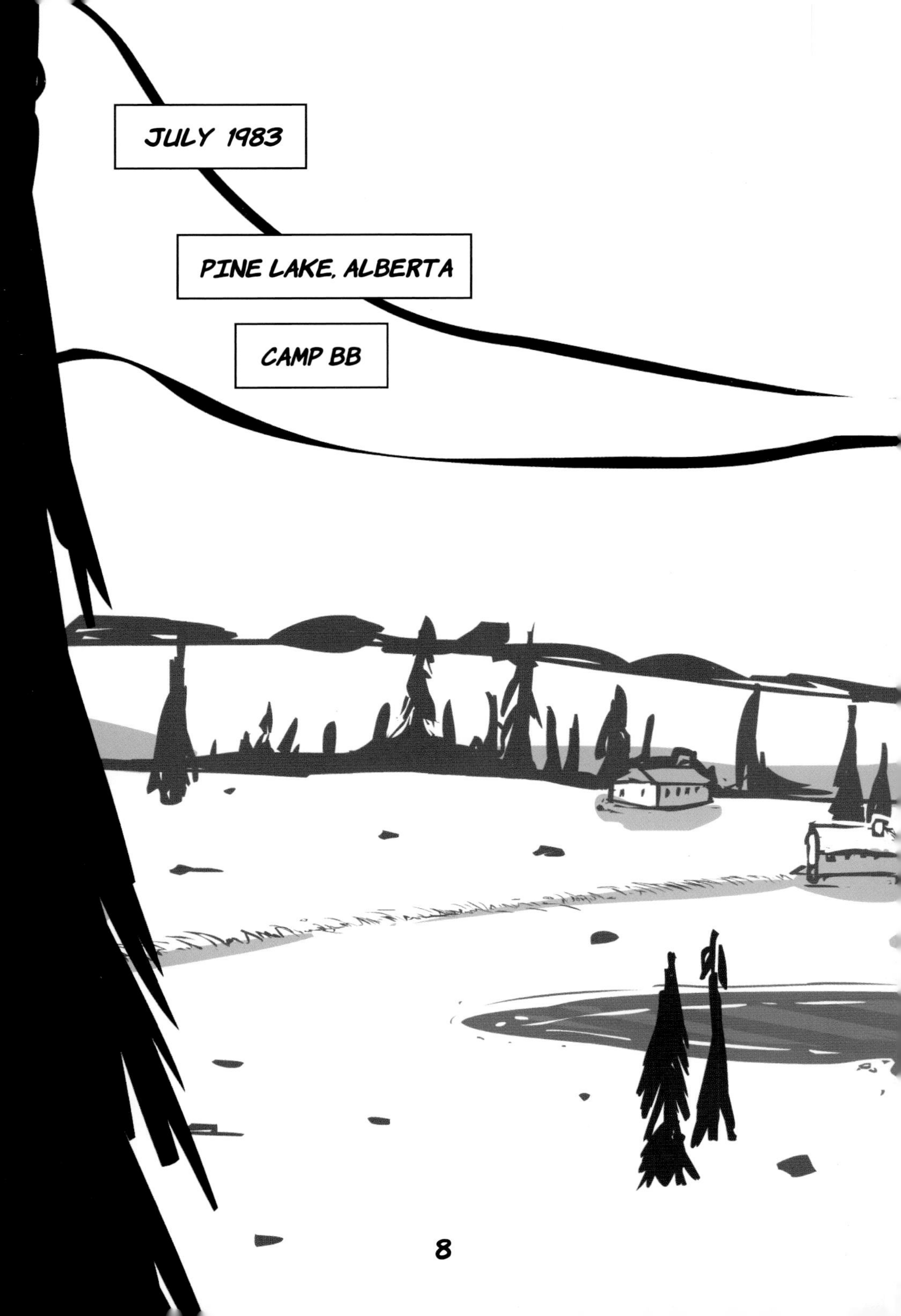
JULY 1983
PINE LAKE, ALBERTA
CAMP BB

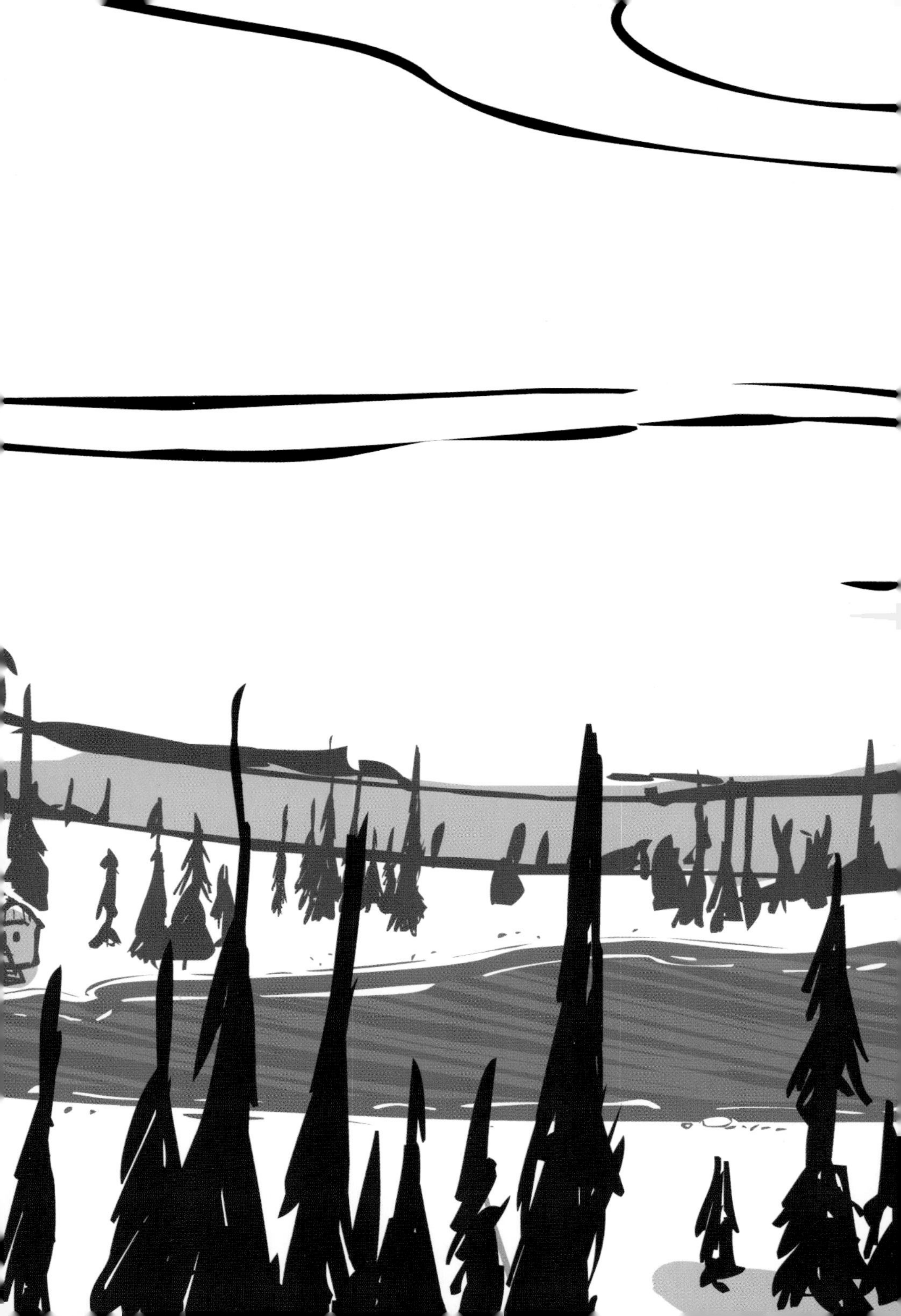

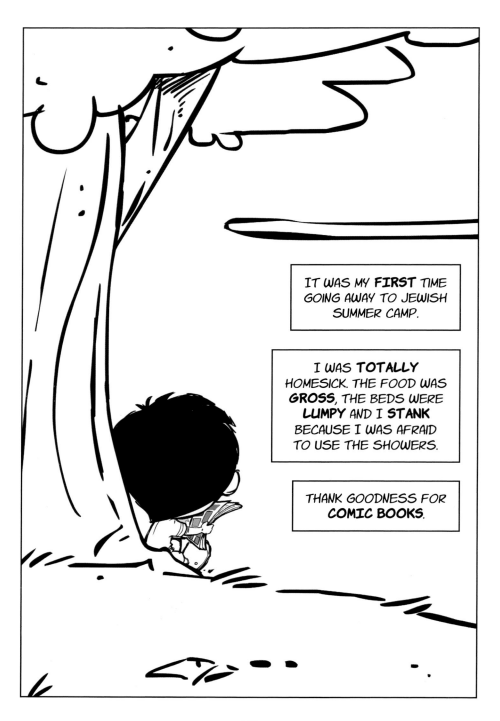

IT WAS MY **FIRST** TIME GOING AWAY TO JEWISH SUMMER CAMP.

I WAS **TOTALLY** HOMESICK. THE FOOD WAS **GROSS**, THE BEDS WERE **LUMPY** AND I **STANK** BECAUSE I WAS AFRAID TO USE THE SHOWERS.

THANK GOODNESS FOR **COMIC BOOKS**.

SUPERMENSCH

18

*MENSCH MEANS "A GOOD PERSON" IN YIDDISH

EVERYONE HAD BROUGHT A FEW FROM HOME.

HEY, HORNHEAD, GUESS WHAT?

GARRR!

SURE, THERE WERE SPORTS TO PLAY, AND LOTS OF FUN ACTIVITIES.

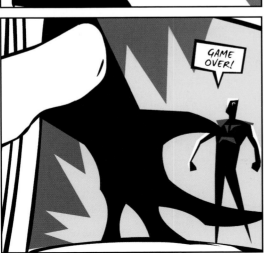

GAME OVER!

BUT, HONESTLY? I JUST WANTED TO BE LEFT ALONE SO I COULD READ **EVERY SINGLE COMIC BOOK** I COULD FIND.

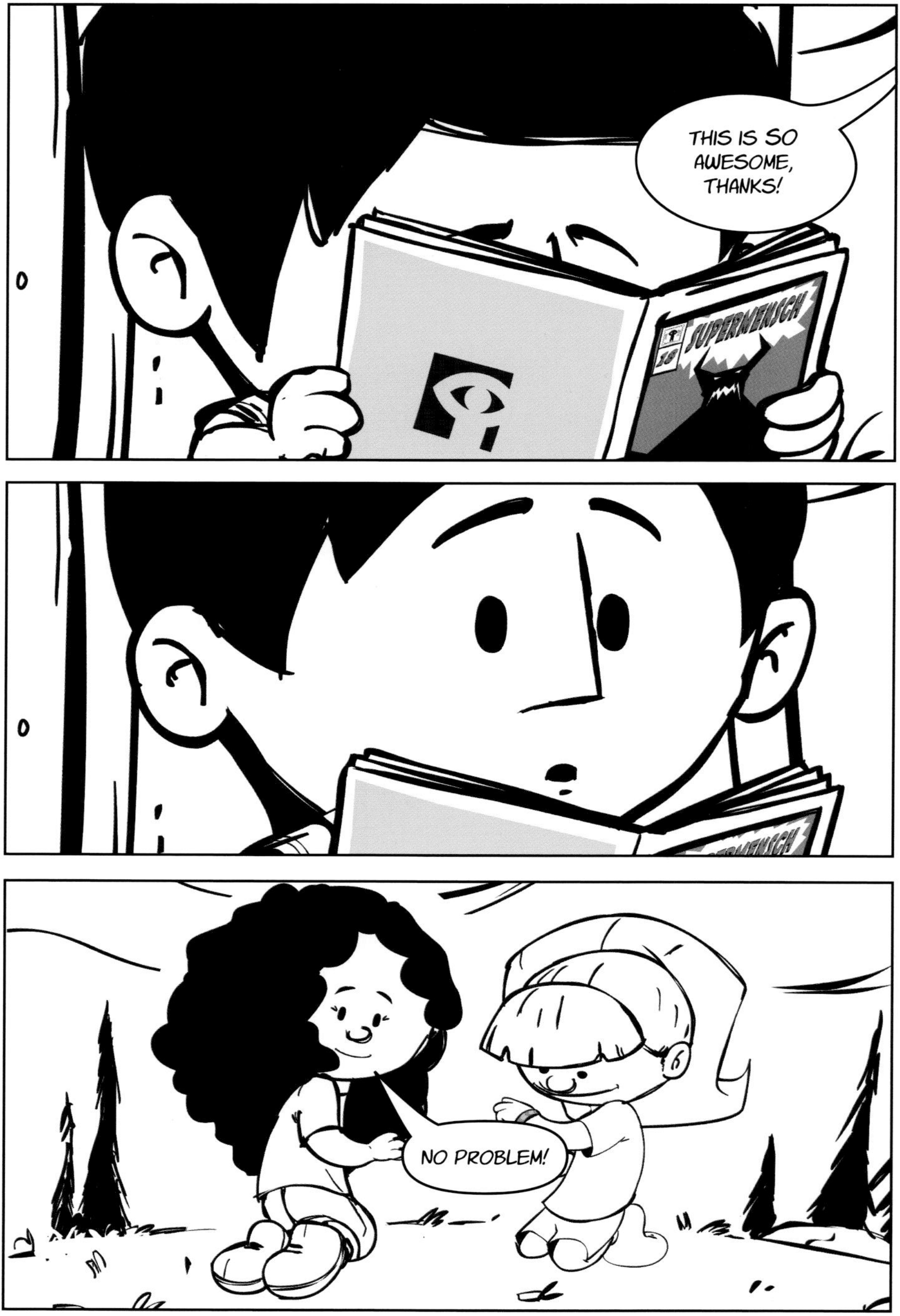
THIS IS SO AWESOME, THANKS!
SUPERMENSCH
NO PROBLEM!

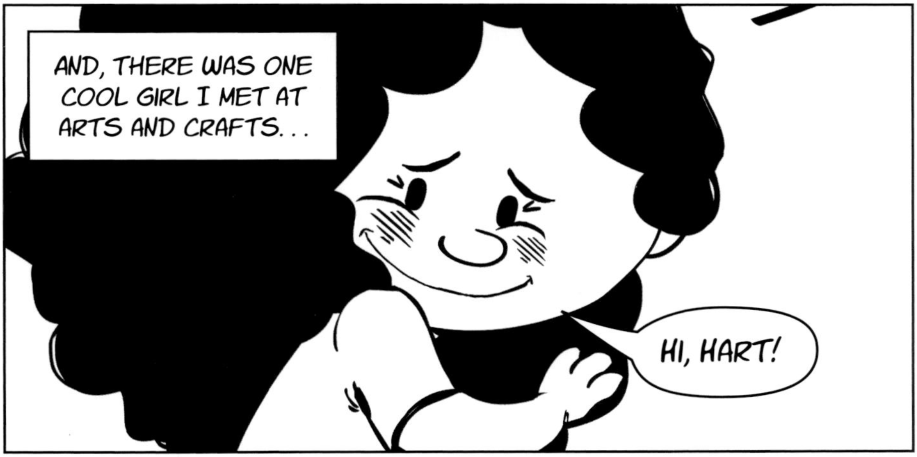
AND, THERE WAS ONE COOL GIRL I MET AT ARTS AND CRAFTS. . .
HI, HART!

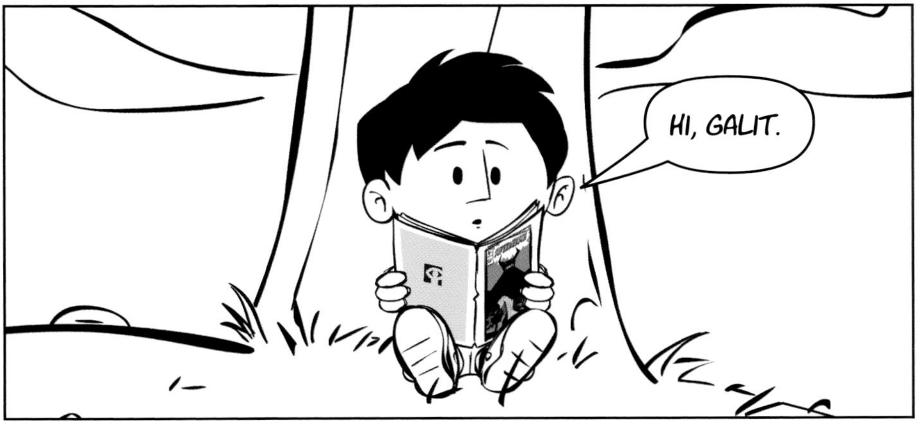
HI, GALIT.

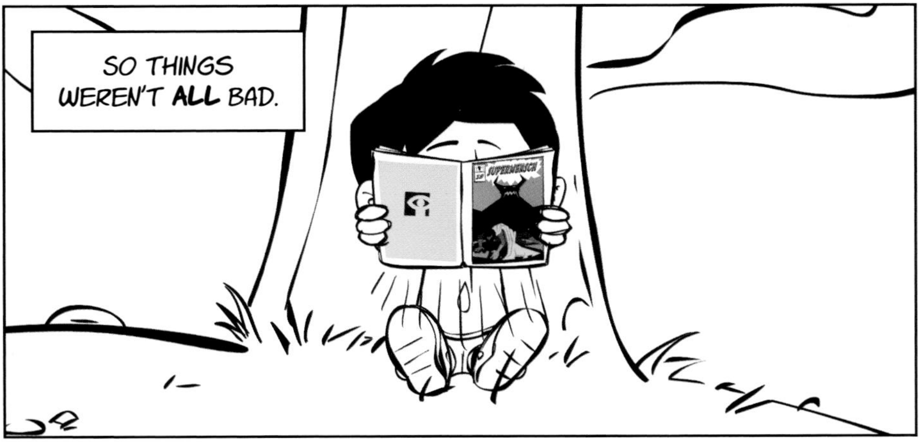
SO THINGS WEREN'T **ALL** BAD.

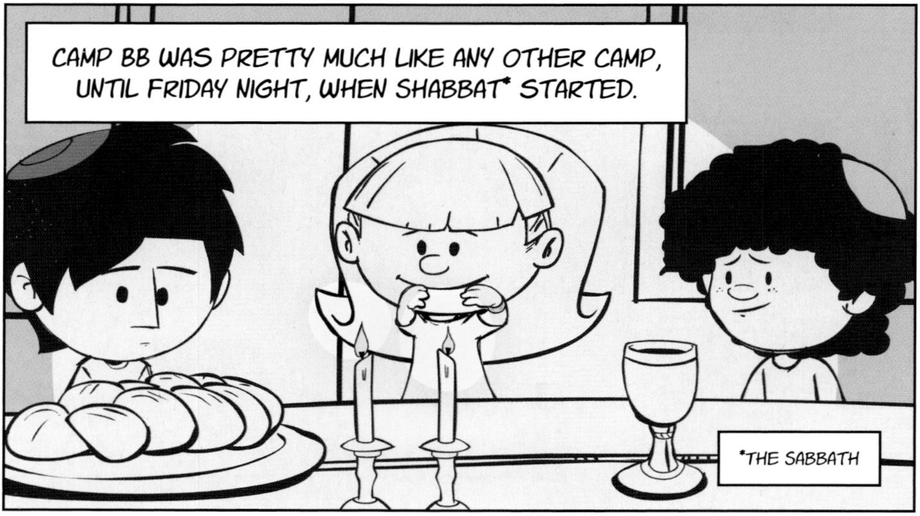
CAMP BB WAS PRETTY MUCH LIKE ANY OTHER CAMP, UNTIL FRIDAY NIGHT, WHEN SHABBAT* STARTED.
*THE SABBATH

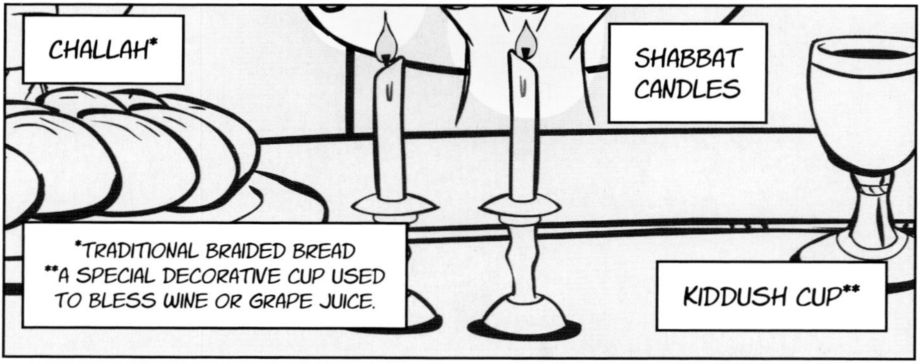
CHALLAH*
SHABBAT CANDLES
*TRADITIONAL BRAIDED BREAD
**A SPECIAL DECORATIVE CUP USED TO BLESS WINE OR GRAPE JUICE.
KIDDUSH CUP**

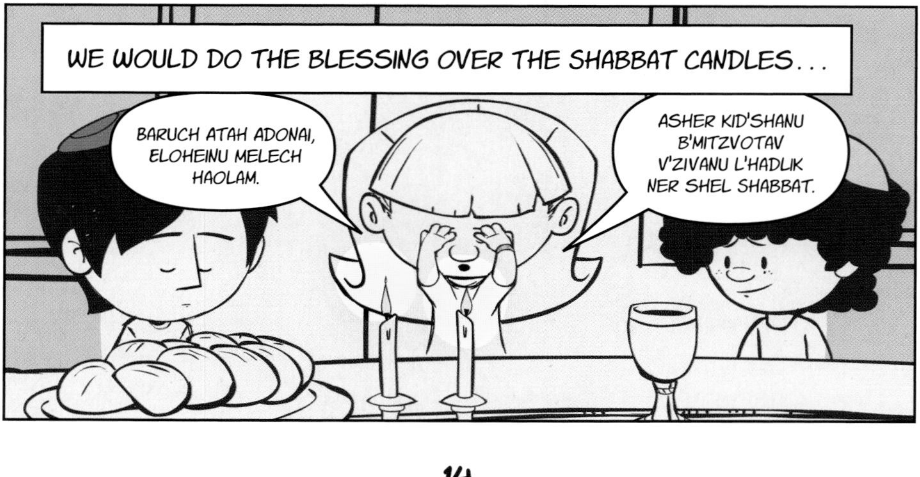
WE WOULD DO THE BLESSING OVER THE SHABBAT CANDLES...
BARUCH ATAH ADONAI, ELOHEINU MELECH HAOLAM.
ASHER KID'SHANU B'MITZVOTAV V'ZIVANU L'HADLIK NER SHEL SHABBAT.

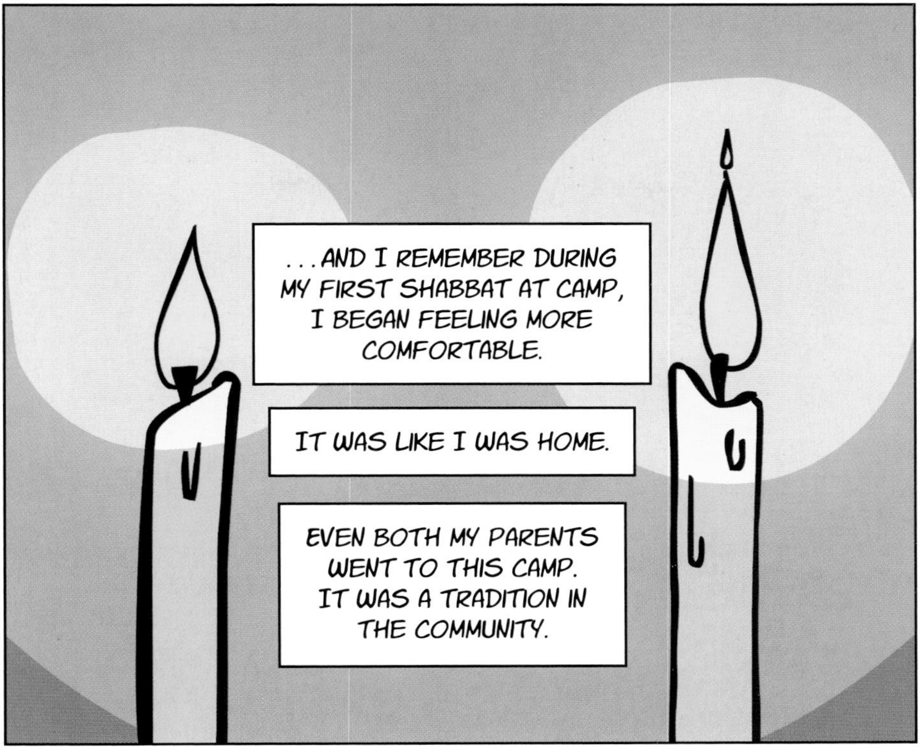
. . . AND I REMEMBER DURING MY FIRST SHABBAT AT CAMP, I BEGAN FEELING MORE COMFORTABLE.
IT WAS LIKE I WAS HOME.
EVEN BOTH MY PARENTS WENT TO THIS CAMP. IT WAS A TRADITION IN THE COMMUNITY.

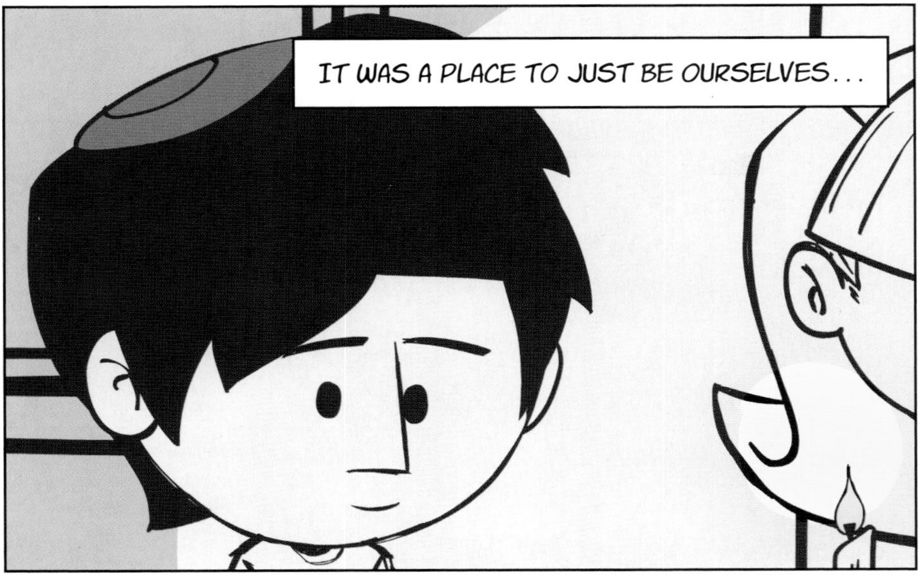
IT WAS A PLACE TO JUST BE OURSELVES . . .

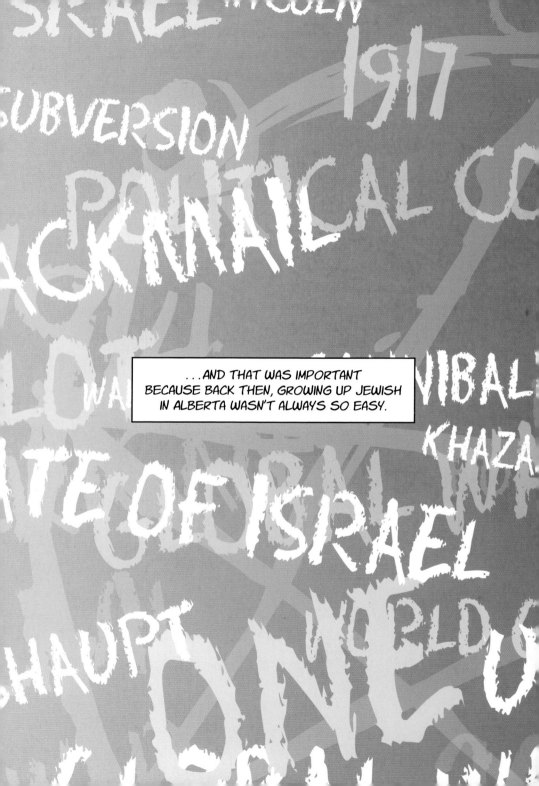

...AND THAT WAS IMPORTANT BECAUSE BACK THEN, GROWING UP JEWISH IN ALBERTA WASN'T ALWAYS SO EASY.

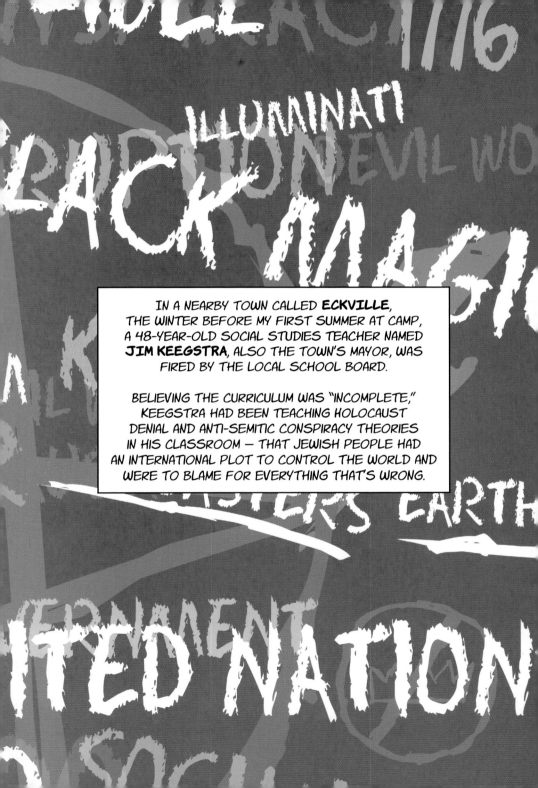

IN A NEARBY TOWN CALLED **ECKVILLE**,
THE WINTER BEFORE MY FIRST SUMMER AT CAMP,
A 48-YEAR-OLD SOCIAL STUDIES TEACHER NAMED
JIM KEEGSTRA, ALSO THE TOWN'S MAYOR, WAS
FIRED BY THE LOCAL SCHOOL BOARD.

BELIEVING THE CURRICULUM WAS "INCOMPLETE,"
KEEGSTRA HAD BEEN TEACHING HOLOCAUST
DENIAL AND ANTI-SEMITIC CONSPIRACY THEORIES
IN HIS CLASSROOM — THAT JEWISH PEOPLE HAD
AN INTERNATIONAL PLOT TO CONTROL THE WORLD AND
WERE TO BLAME FOR EVERYTHING THAT'S WRONG.

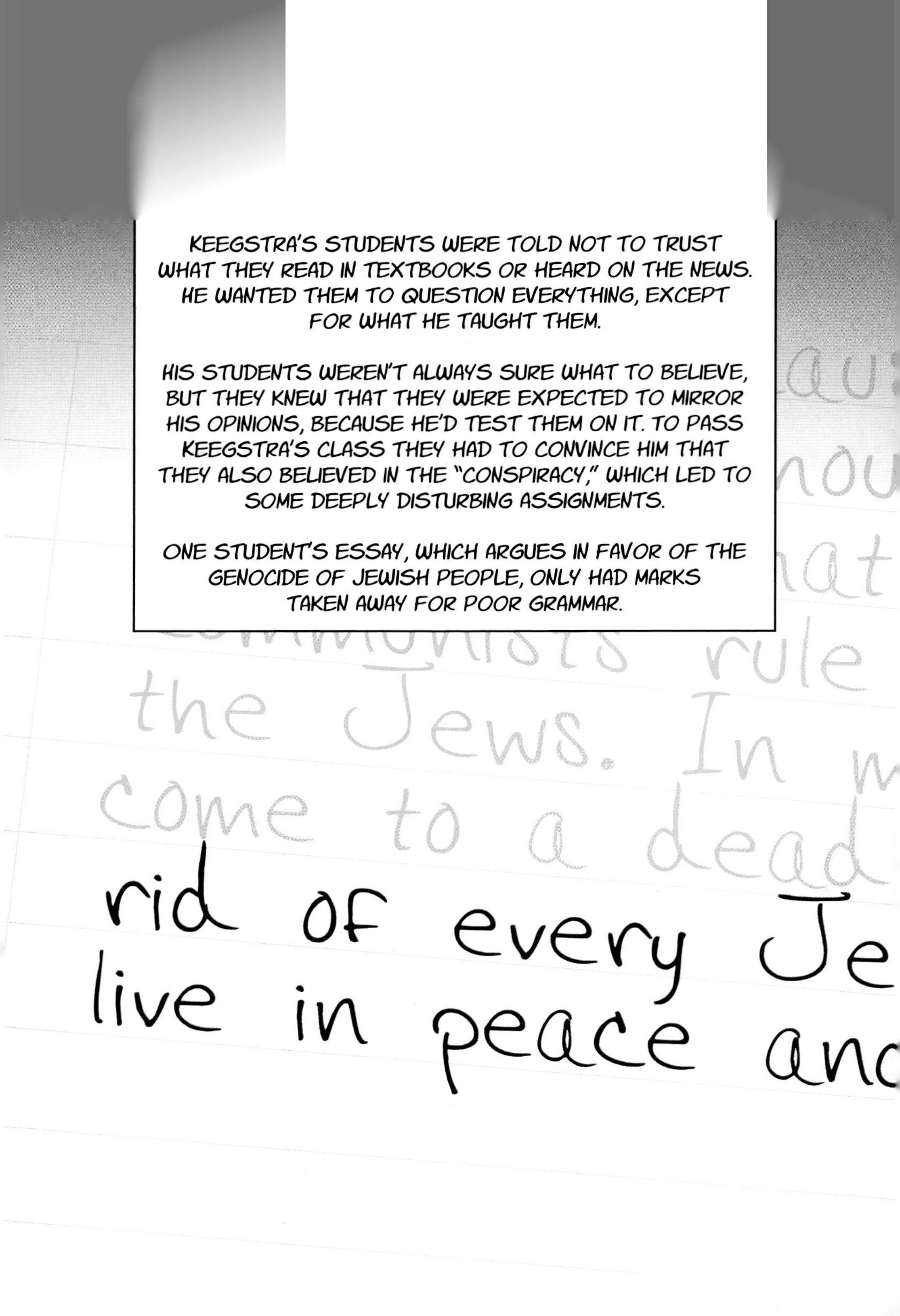
KEEGSTRA'S STUDENTS WERE TOLD NOT TO TRUST WHAT THEY READ IN TEXTBOOKS OR HEARD ON THE NEWS. HE WANTED THEM TO QUESTION EVERYTHING, EXCEPT FOR WHAT HE TAUGHT THEM.
HIS STUDENTS WEREN'T ALWAYS SURE WHAT TO BELIEVE, BUT THEY KNEW THAT THEY WERE EXPECTED TO MIRROR HIS OPINIONS, BECAUSE HE'D TEST THEM ON IT. TO PASS KEEGSTRA'S CLASS THEY HAD TO CONVINCE HIM THAT THEY ALSO BELIEVED IN THE "CONSPIRACY," WHICH LED TO SOME DEEPLY DISTURBING ASSIGNMENTS.
ONE STUDENT'S ESSAY, WHICH ARGUES IN FAVOR OF THE GENOCIDE OF JEWISH PEOPLE, ONLY HAD MARKS TAKEN AWAY FOR POOR GRAMMAR.
rule
the Jews. In
come to a dead
rid of every Je
live in peace an

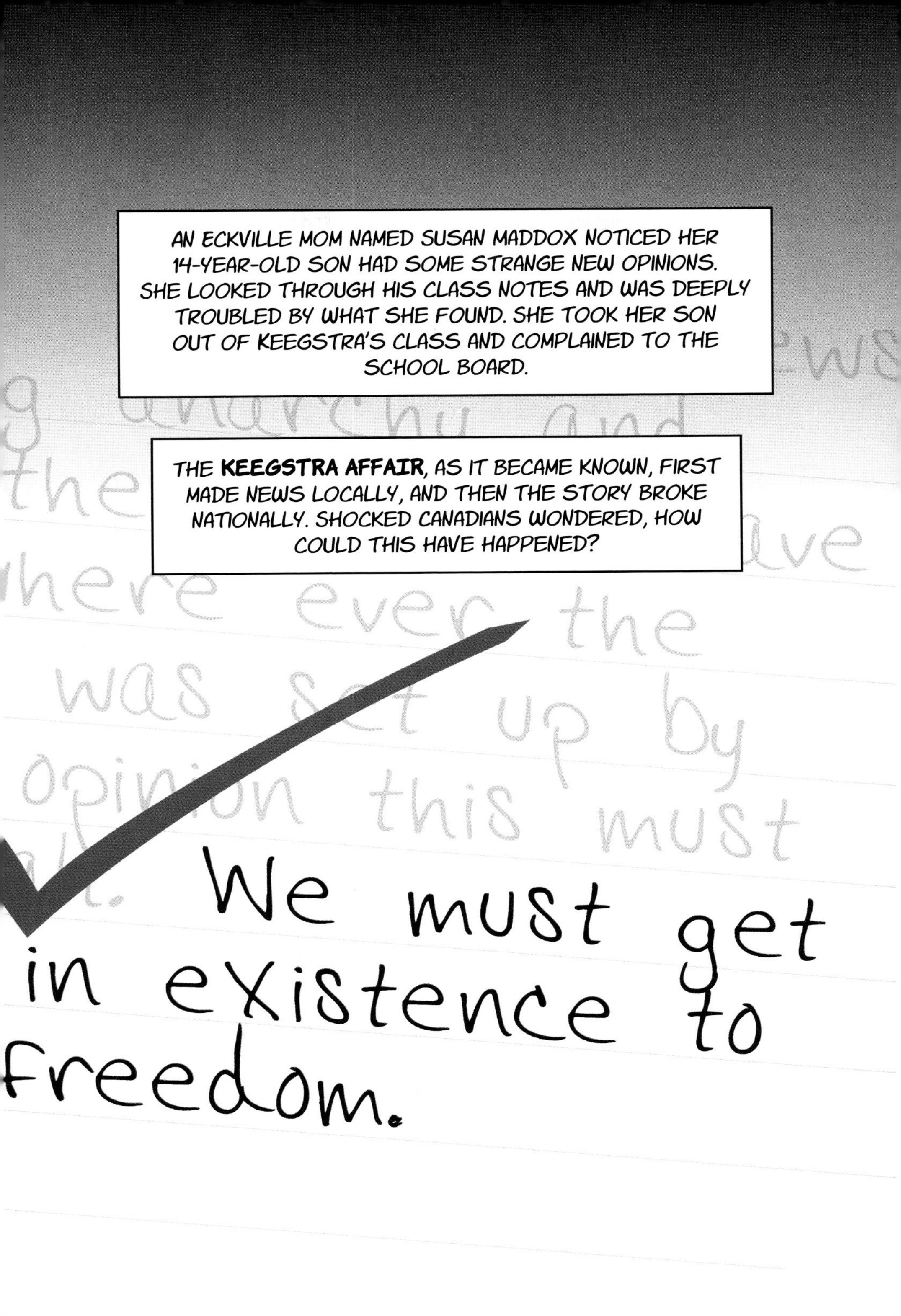
AN ECKVILLE MOM NAMED SUSAN MADDOX NOTICED HER 14-YEAR-OLD SON HAD SOME STRANGE NEW OPINIONS. SHE LOOKED THROUGH HIS CLASS NOTES AND WAS DEEPLY TROUBLED BY WHAT SHE FOUND. SHE TOOK HER SON OUT OF KEEGSTRA'S CLASS AND COMPLAINED TO THE SCHOOL BOARD.
THE **KEEGSTRA AFFAIR**, AS IT BECAME KNOWN, FIRST MADE NEWS LOCALLY, AND THEN THE STORY BROKE NATIONALLY. SHOCKED CANADIANS WONDERED, HOW COULD THIS HAVE HAPPENED?
We must get
in existence to
freedom.

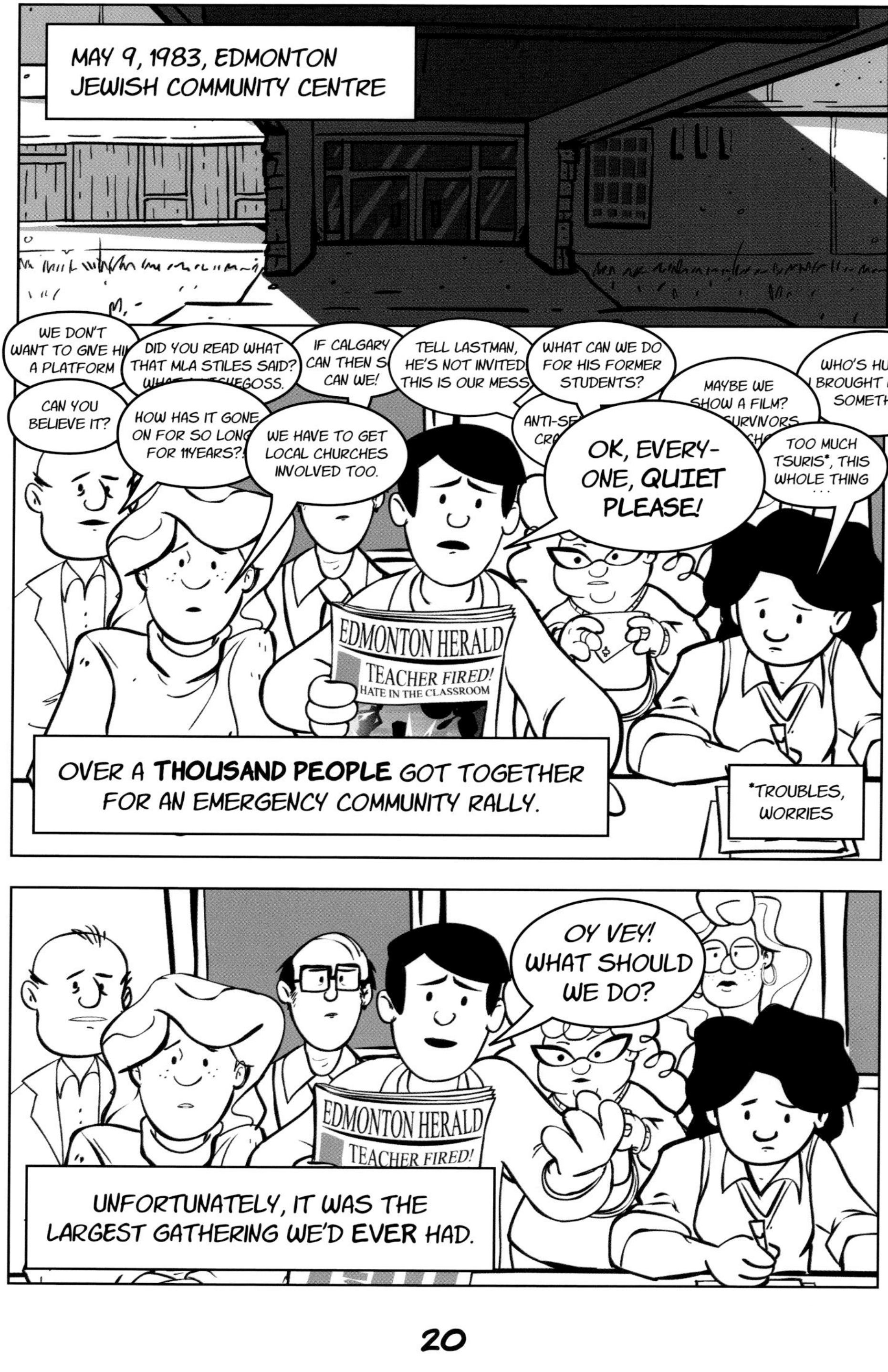
MAY 9, 1983, EDMONTON JEWISH COMMUNITY CENTRE
WE DON'T WANT TO GIVE HI A PLATFORM
DID YOU READ WHAT THAT MLA STILES SAID?
IF CALGARY CAN THEN S CAN WE!
TELL LASTMAN, HE'S NOT INVITED! THIS IS OUR MESS
WHAT CAN WE DO FOR HIS FORMER STUDENTS?
WHO'S HUNGRY? I BROUGHT A LITTLE SOMETHING...
CAN YOU BELIEVE IT?
HOW HAS IT GONE ON FOR SO LONG FOR 11YEARS?!
WE HAVE TO GET LOCAL CHURCHES INVOLVED TOO.
MAYBE WE SHOW A FILM? SURVIVORS
OK, EVERY-ONE, QUIET PLEASE!
TOO MUCH TSURIS*, THIS WHOLE THING ...
EDMONTON HERALD
TEACHER FIRED!
HATE IN THE CLASSROOM
OVER A THOUSAND PEOPLE GOT TOGETHER FOR AN EMERGENCY COMMUNITY RALLY.
*TROUBLES, WORRIES
OY VEY! WHAT SHOULD WE DO?
EDMONTON HERALD
TEACHER FIRED!
UNFORTUNATELY, IT WAS THE LARGEST GATHERING WE'D EVER HAD.

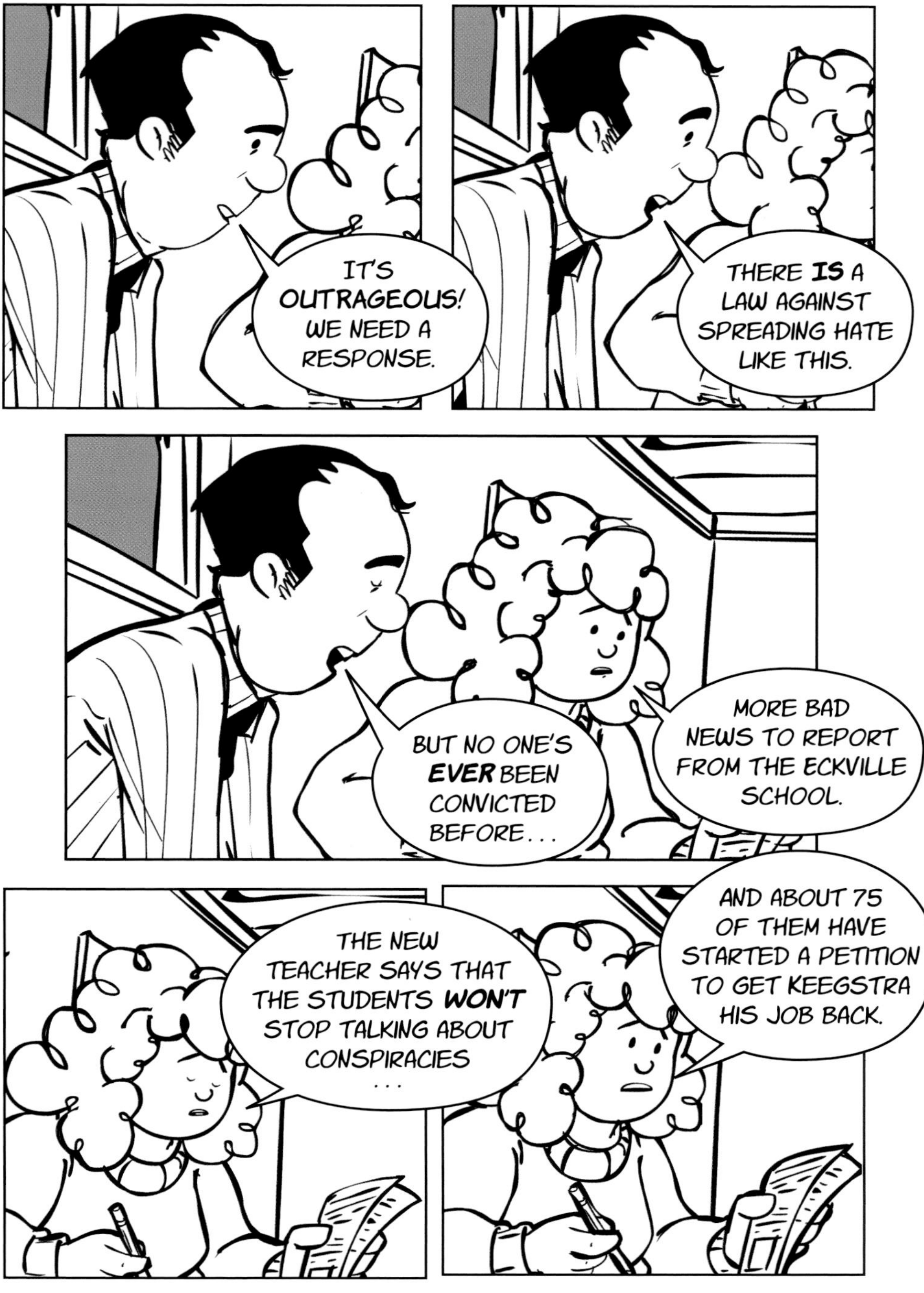
IT'S **OUTRAGEOUS!** WE NEED A RESPONSE.
THERE **IS** A LAW AGAINST SPREADING HATE LIKE THIS.
BUT NO ONE'S **EVER** BEEN CONVICTED BEFORE . . .
MORE BAD NEWS TO REPORT FROM THE ECKVILLE SCHOOL.
THE NEW TEACHER SAYS THAT THE STUDENTS **WON'T** STOP TALKING ABOUT CONSPIRACIES . . .
AND ABOUT 75 OF THEM HAVE STARTED A PETITION TO GET KEEGSTRA HIS JOB BACK.

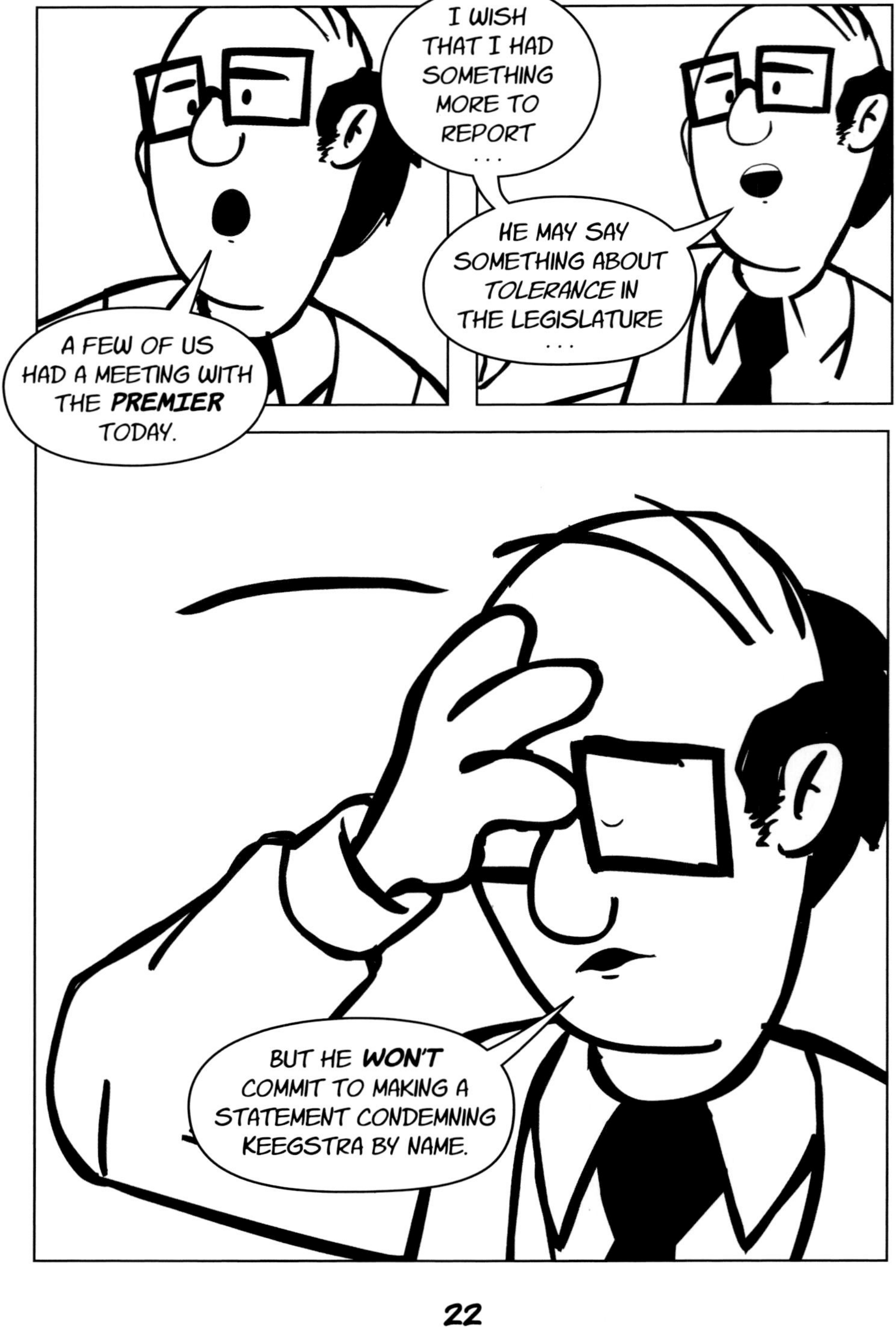
A FEW OF US HAD A MEETING WITH THE **PREMIER** TODAY.
I WISH THAT I HAD SOMETHING MORE TO REPORT . . .
HE MAY SAY SOMETHING ABOUT *TOLERANCE* IN THE LEGISLATURE . . .
BUT HE **WON'T** COMMIT TO MAKING A STATEMENT CONDEMNING KEEGSTRA BY NAME.

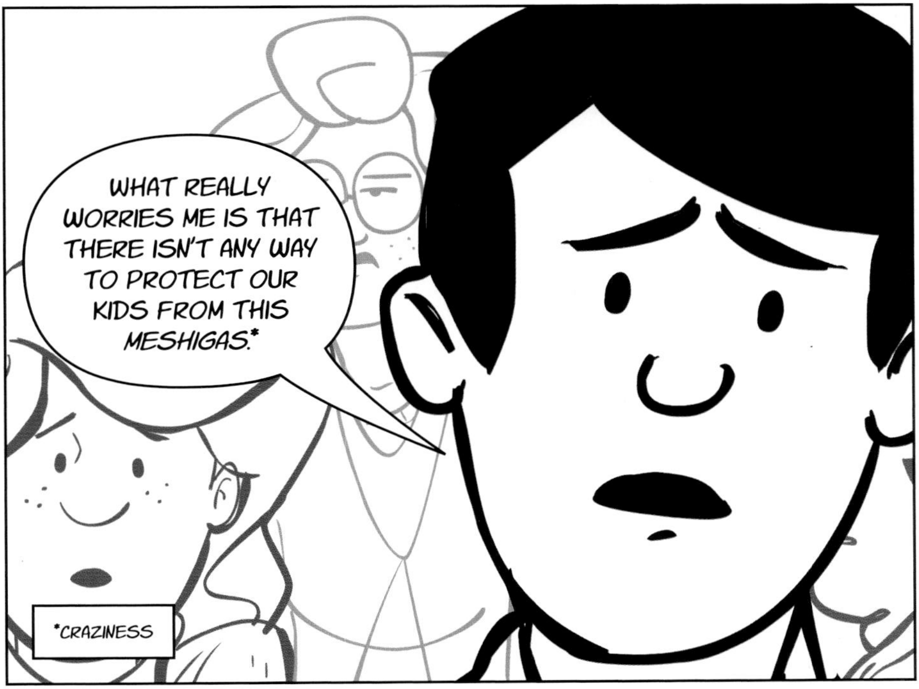
WHAT REALLY WORRIES ME IS THAT THERE ISN'T ANY WAY TO PROTECT OUR KIDS FROM THIS *MESHIGAS.**
*CRAZINESS

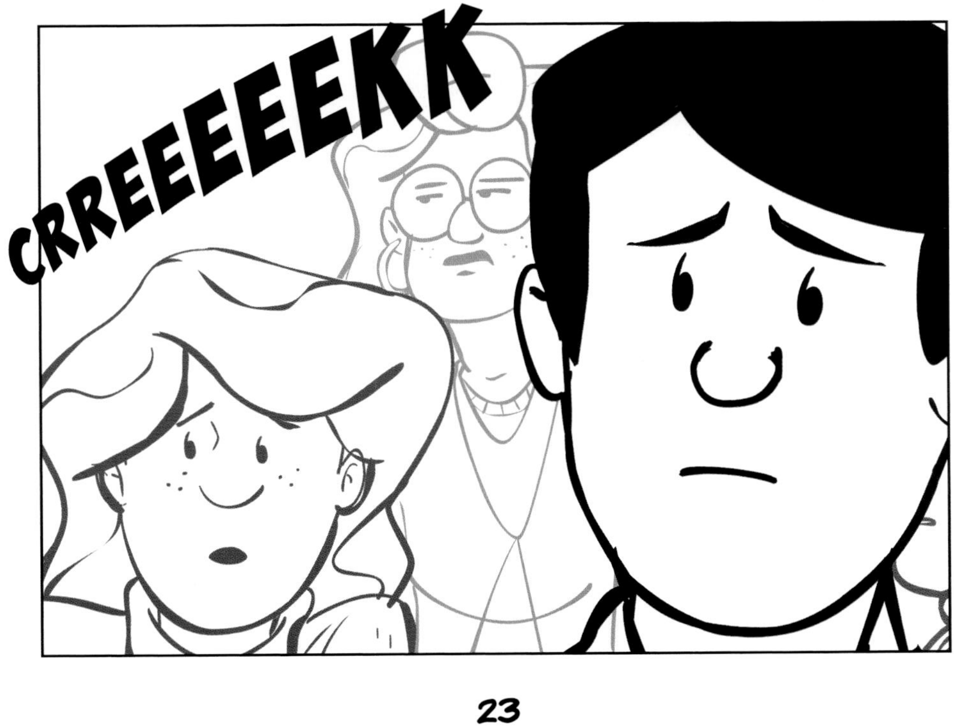
CRREEEEEEKK

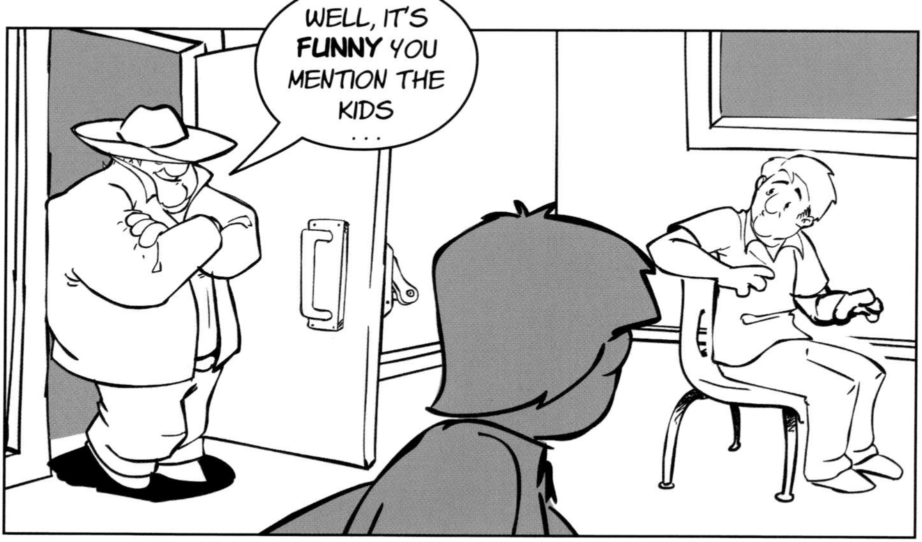
WELL, IT'S **FUNNY** YOU MENTION THE KIDS . . .

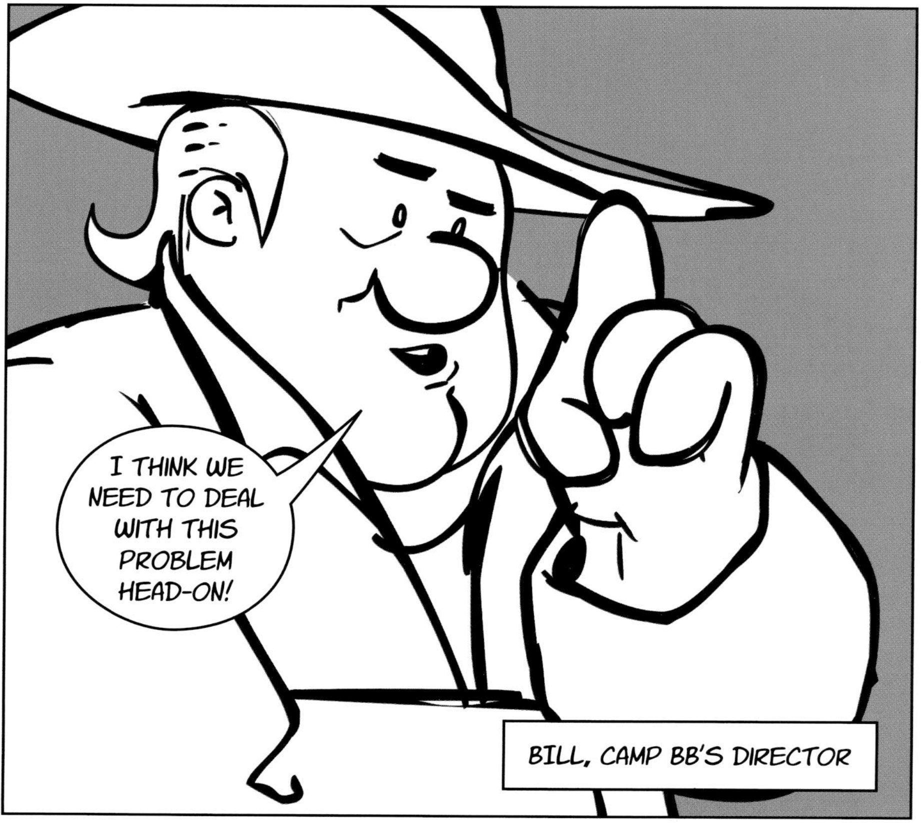
I THINK WE NEED TO DEAL WITH THIS PROBLEM HEAD-ON!
BILL, CAMP BB'S DIRECTOR

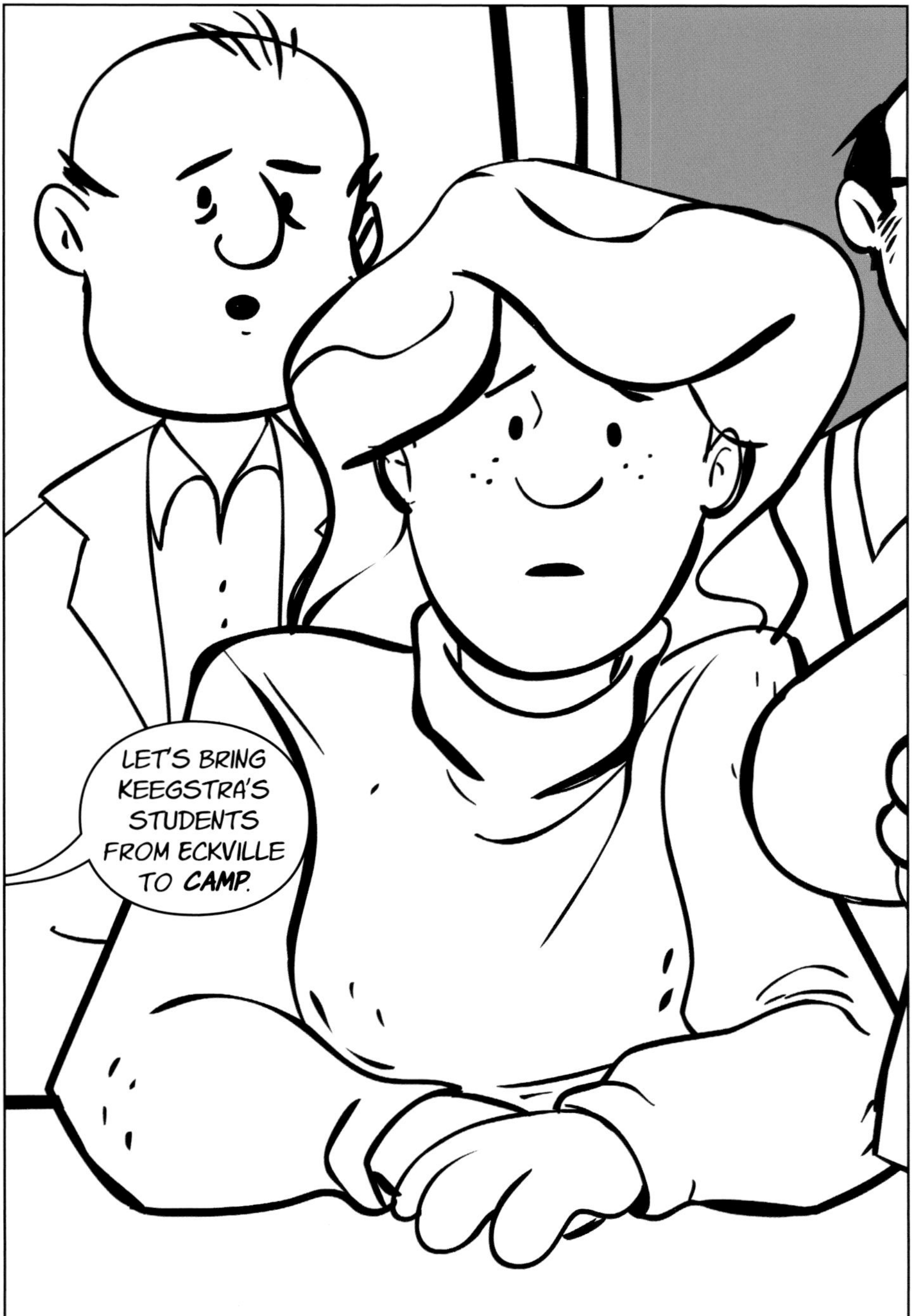
LET'S BRING KEEGSTRA'S STUDENTS FROM ECKVILLE TO **CAMP**.

JULY 9, 1983, CAMP BB
THIS IS A FRIENDSHIP BRACELET.
YOU'RE SUPPOSED TO MAKE A WISH NOW . . .
RIGHT NOW?
. . . THEN WHEN THE BRACELET FALLS OFF . . .
. . . THE WISH WILL COME TRUE.
I PROBABLY WISHED FOR ANOTHER WAYNE GRETZKY ROOKIE CARD . . .
. . . BUT I SHOULD HAVE WISHED TO **FREEZE TIME** –

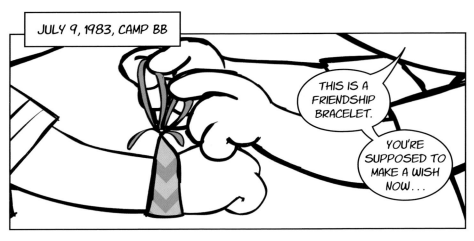

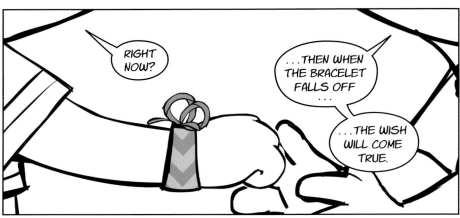

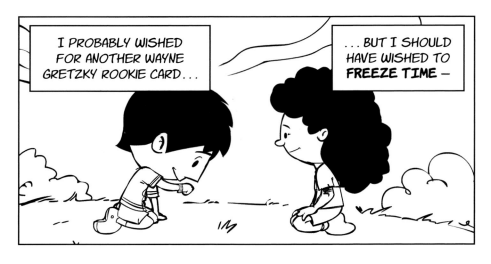

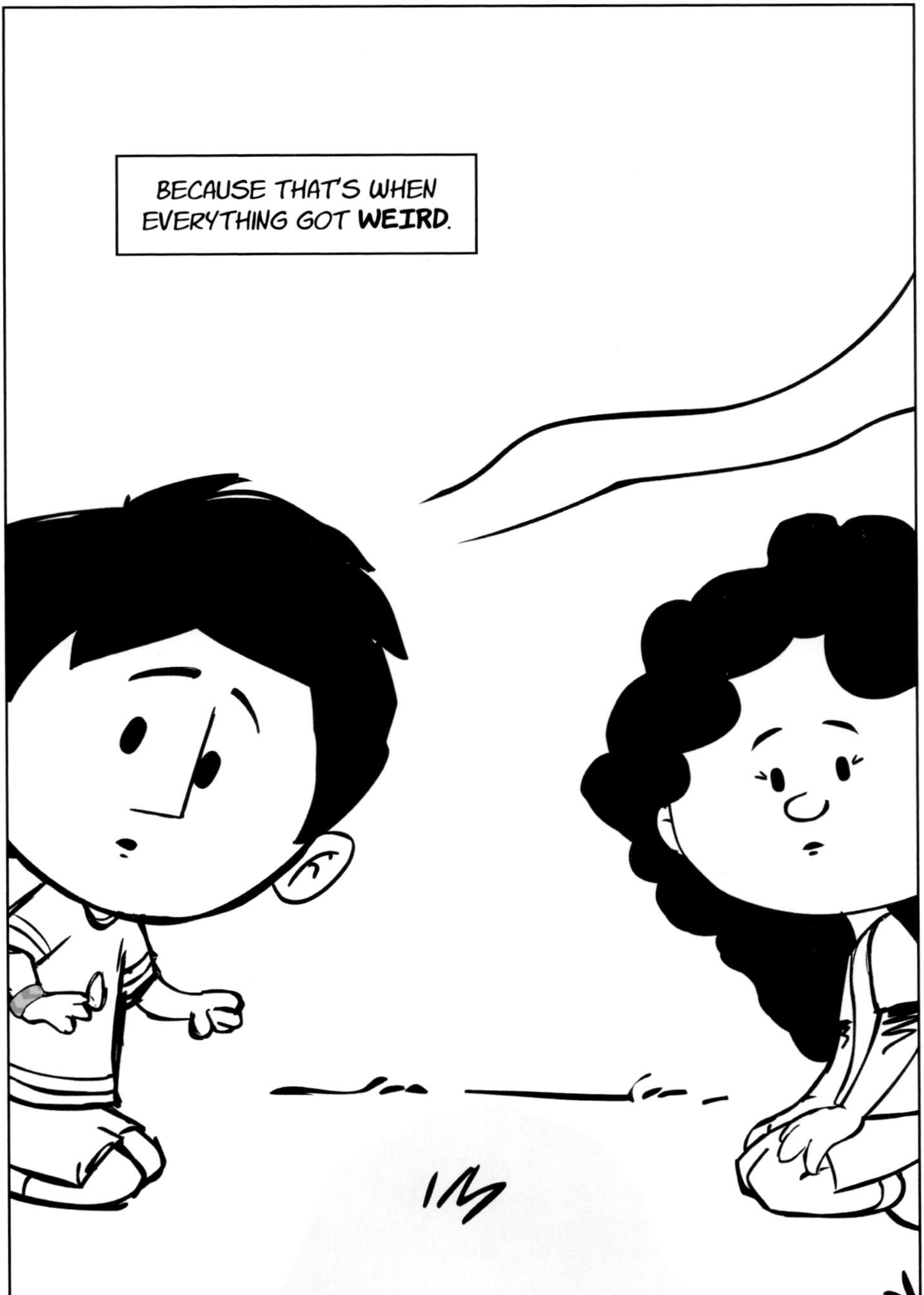
BECAUSE THAT'S WHEN EVERYTHING GOT **WEIRD**.

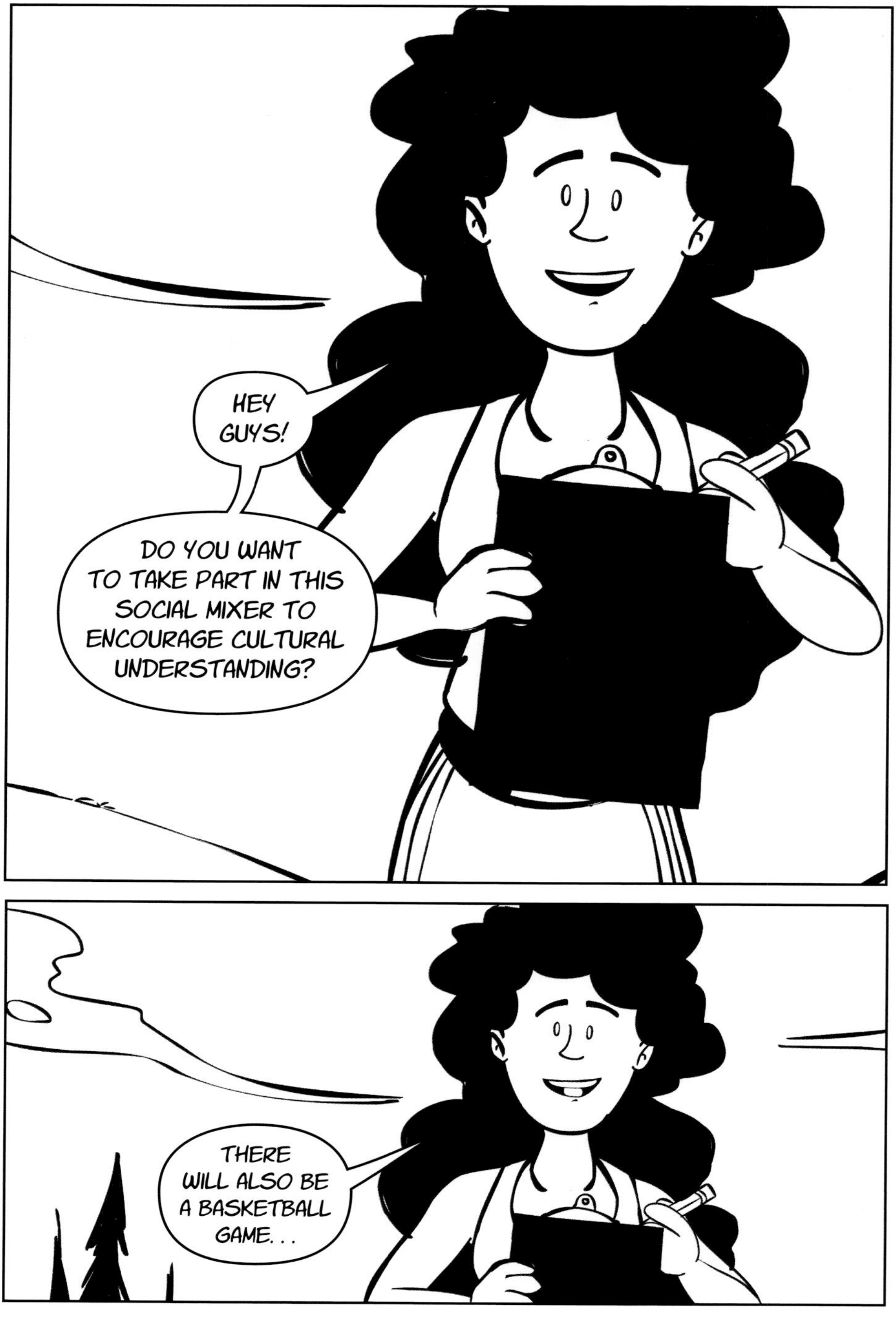
HEY GUYS!
DO YOU WANT TO TAKE PART IN THIS SOCIAL MIXER TO ENCOURAGE CULTURAL UNDERSTANDING?
THERE WILL ALSO BE A BASKETBALL GAME. . .

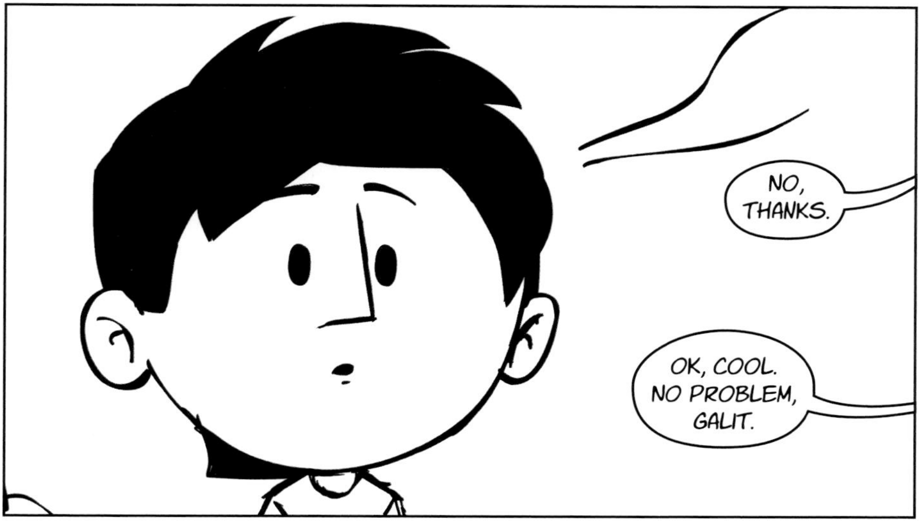
NO, THANKS.
OK, COOL. NO PROBLEM, GALIT.

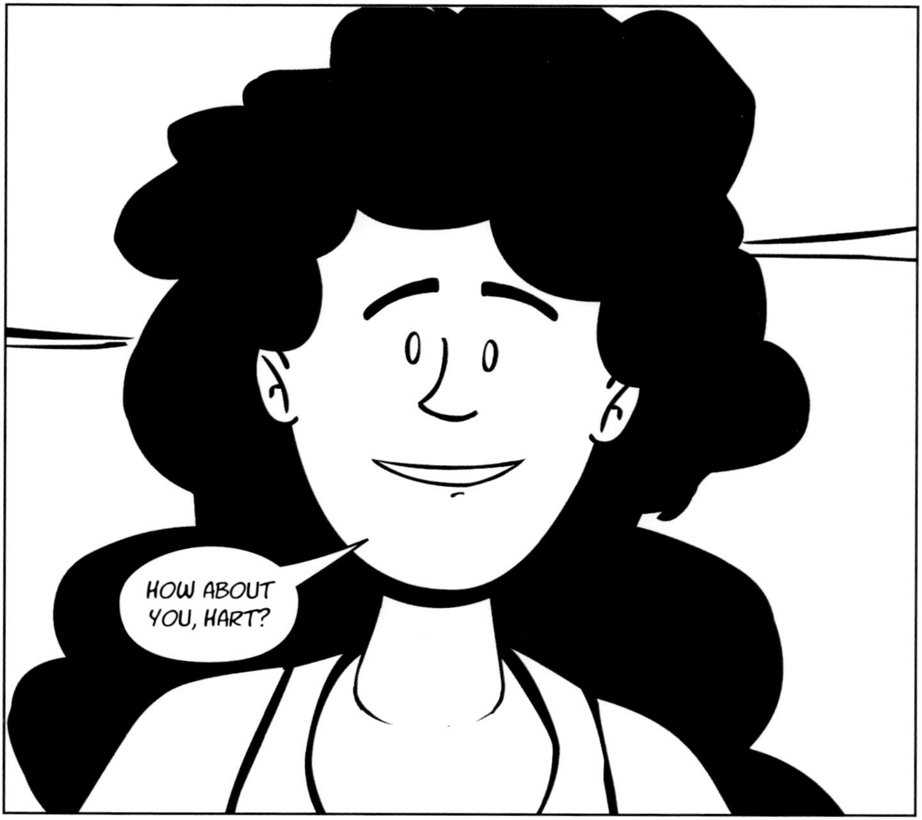
HOW ABOUT YOU, HART?

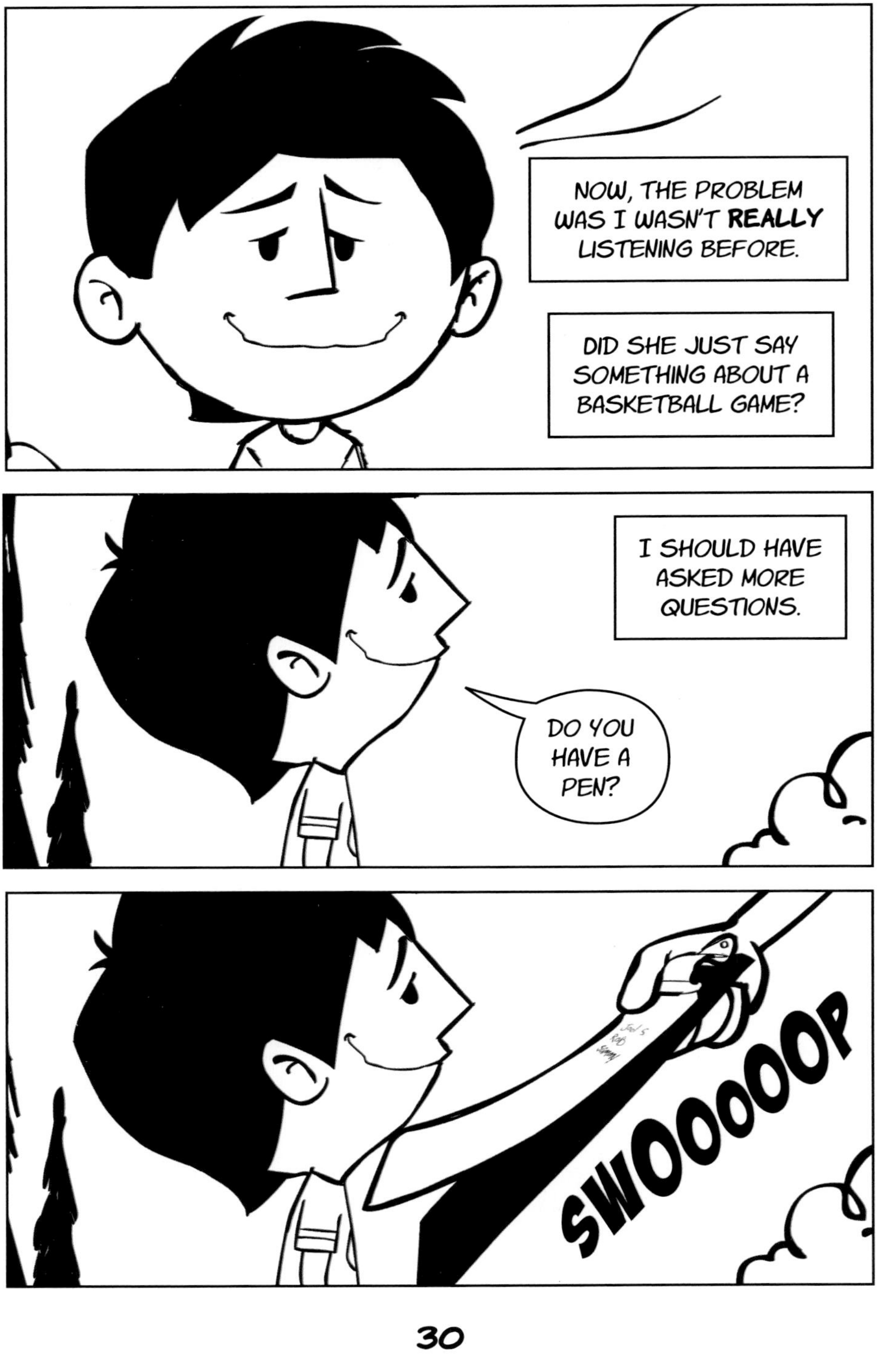
NOW, THE PROBLEM WAS I WASN'T **REALLY** LISTENING BEFORE.
DID SHE JUST SAY SOMETHING ABOUT A BASKETBALL GAME?
I SHOULD HAVE ASKED MORE QUESTIONS.
DO YOU HAVE A PEN?
SWOOOOOP

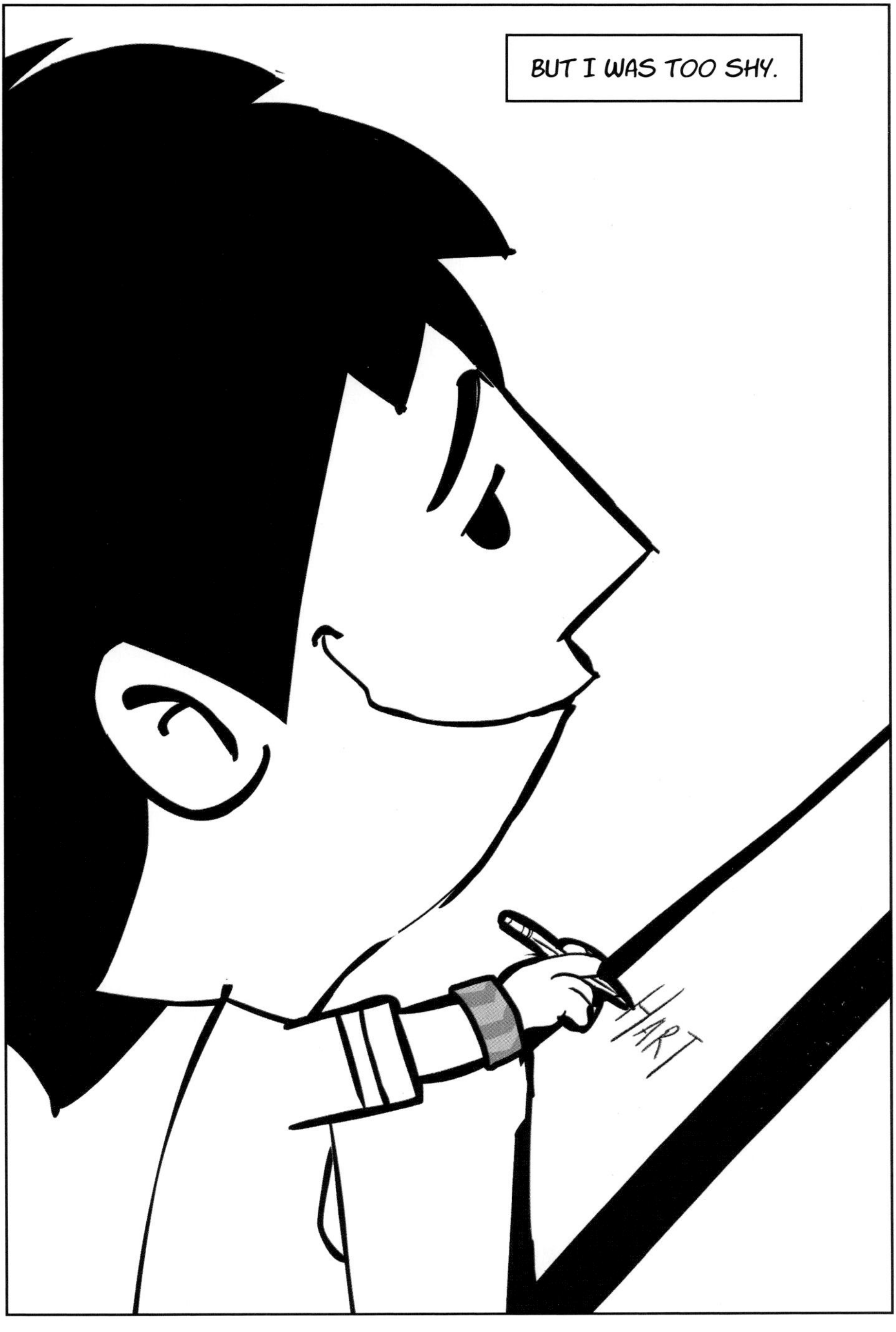
BUT I WAS TOO SHY.
HART

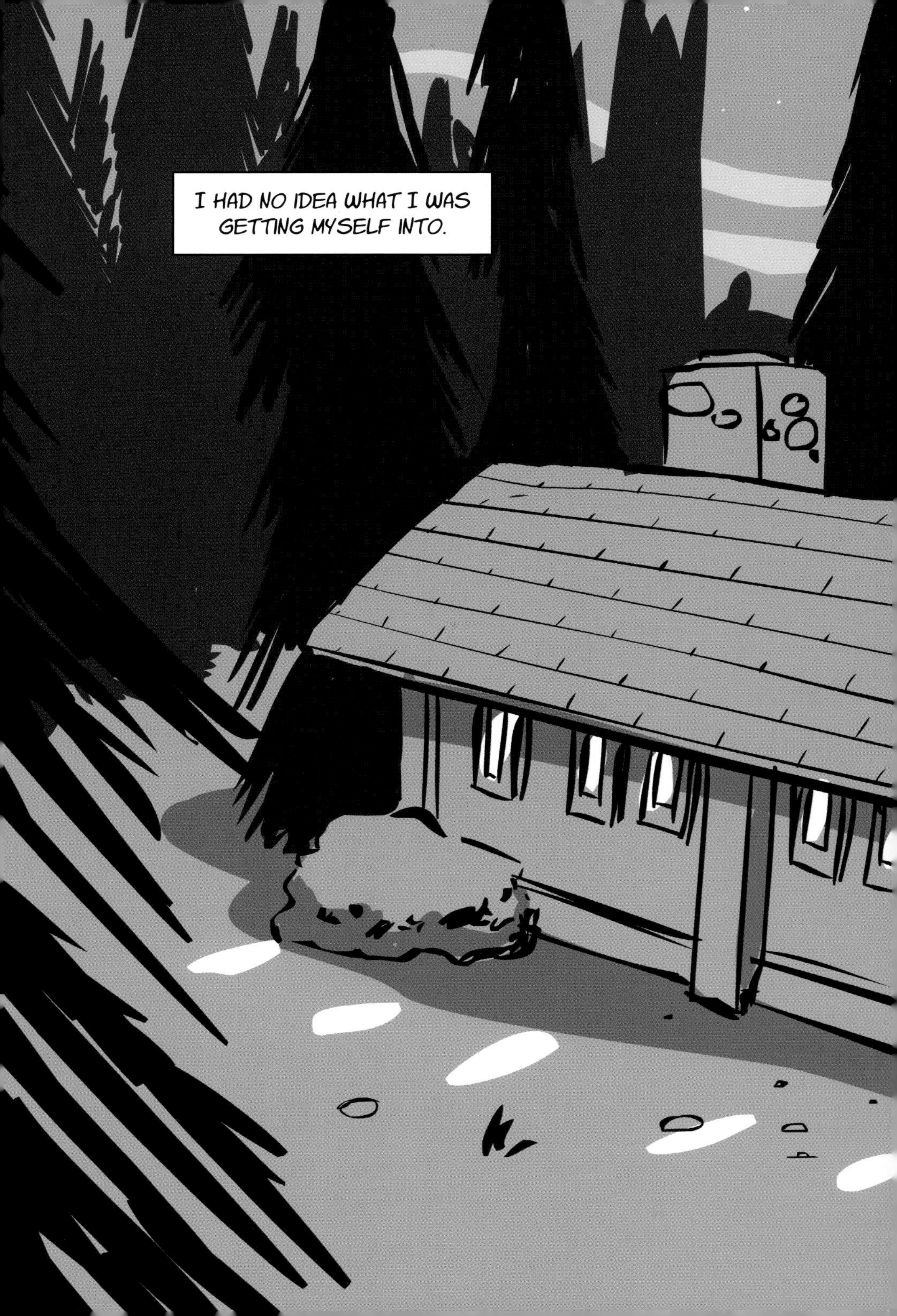
I HAD NO IDEA WHAT I WAS GETTING MYSELF INTO.

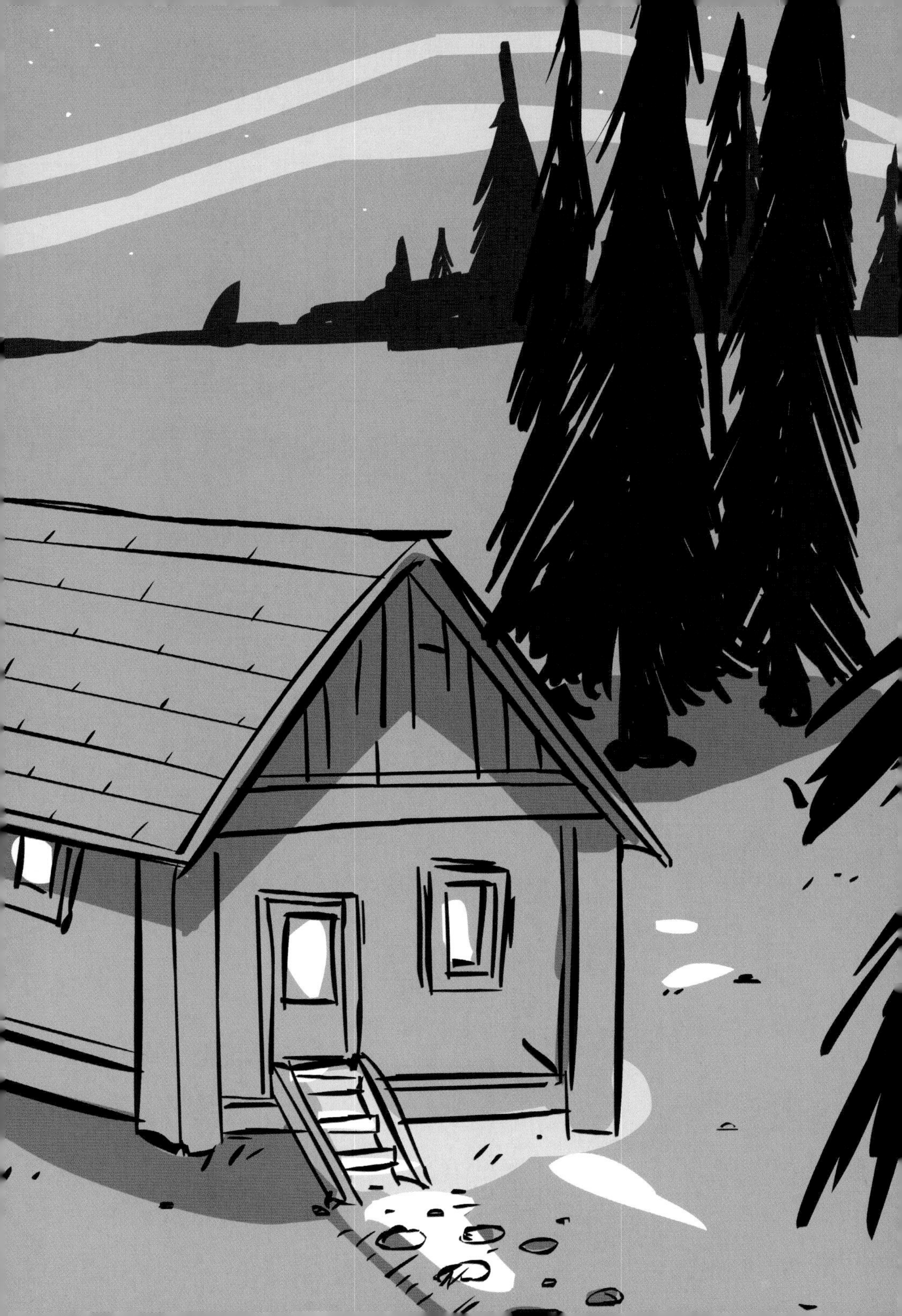

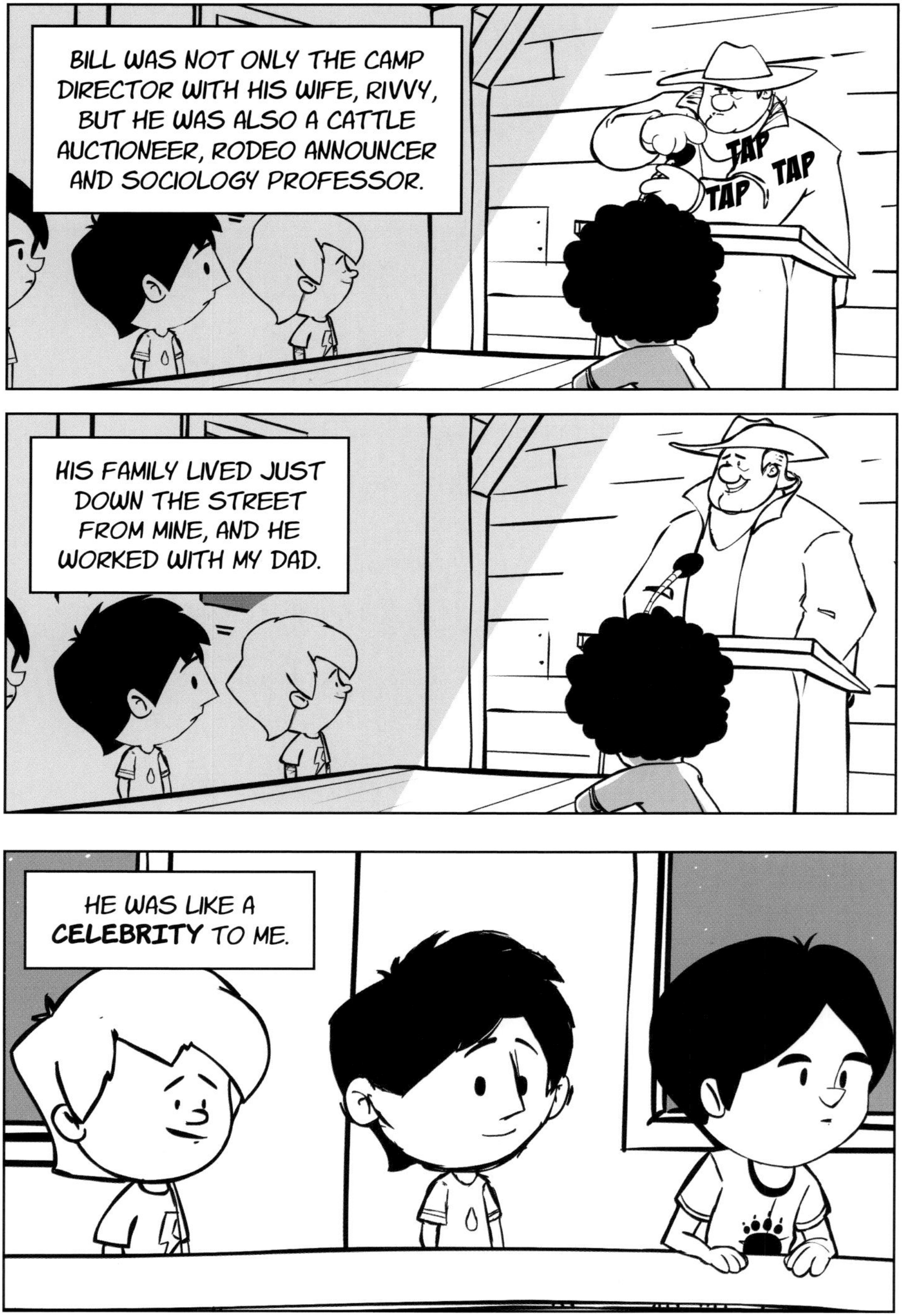
BILL WAS NOT ONLY THE CAMP DIRECTOR WITH HIS WIFE, RIVVY, BUT HE WAS ALSO A CATTLE AUCTIONEER, RODEO ANNOUNCER AND SOCIOLOGY PROFESSOR.
TAP
TAP
TAP
HIS FAMILY LIVED JUST DOWN THE STREET FROM MINE, AND HE WORKED WITH MY DAD.
HE WAS LIKE A **CELEBRITY** TO ME.

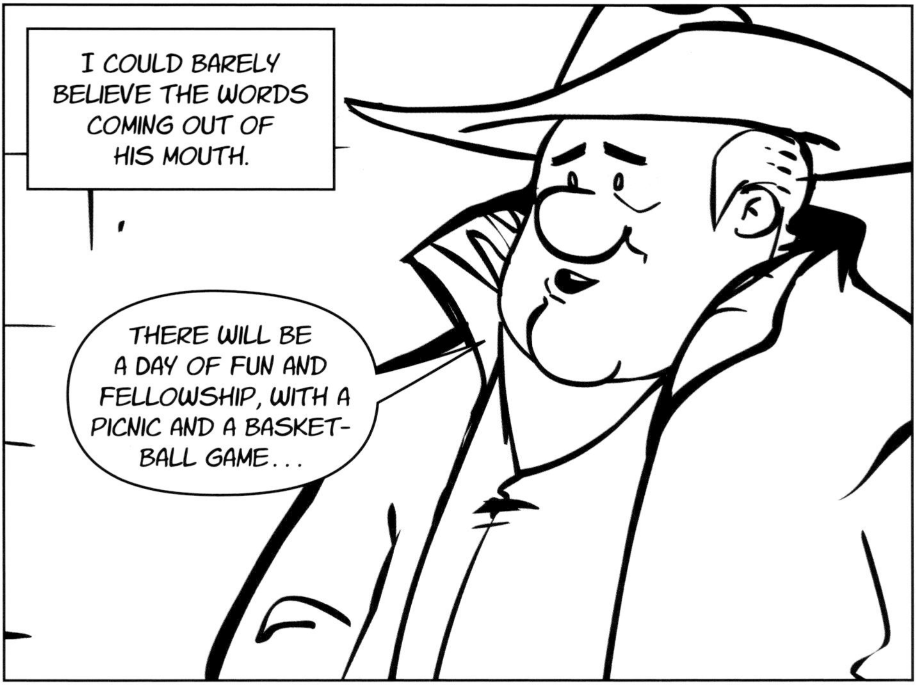
I COULD BARELY BELIEVE THE WORDS COMING OUT OF HIS MOUTH.
THERE WILL BE A DAY OF FUN AND FELLOWSHIP, WITH A PICNIC AND A BASKET-BALL GAME...

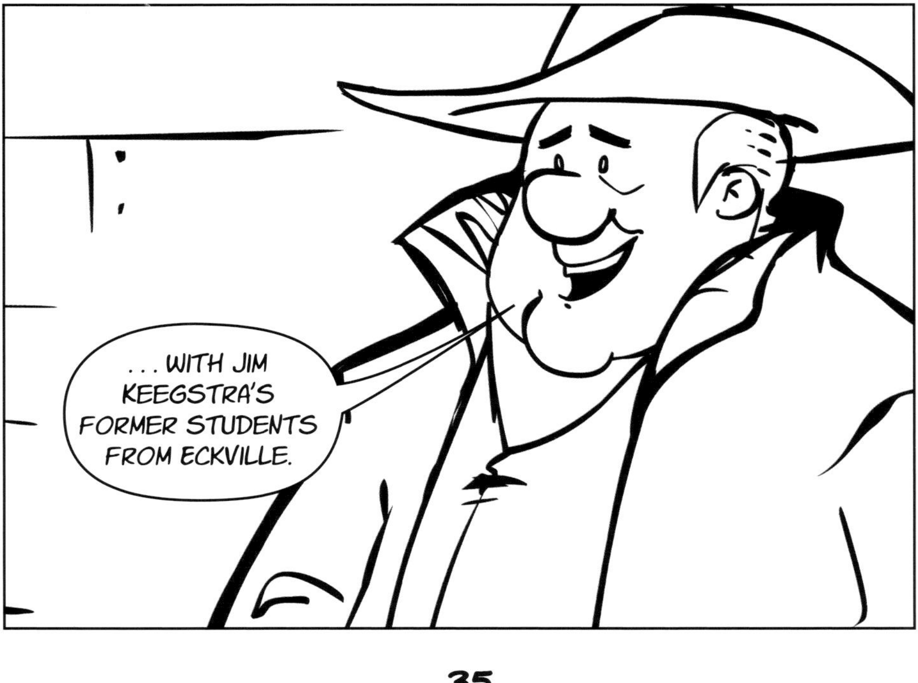
...WITH JIM KEEGSTRA'S FORMER STUDENTS FROM ECKVILLE.

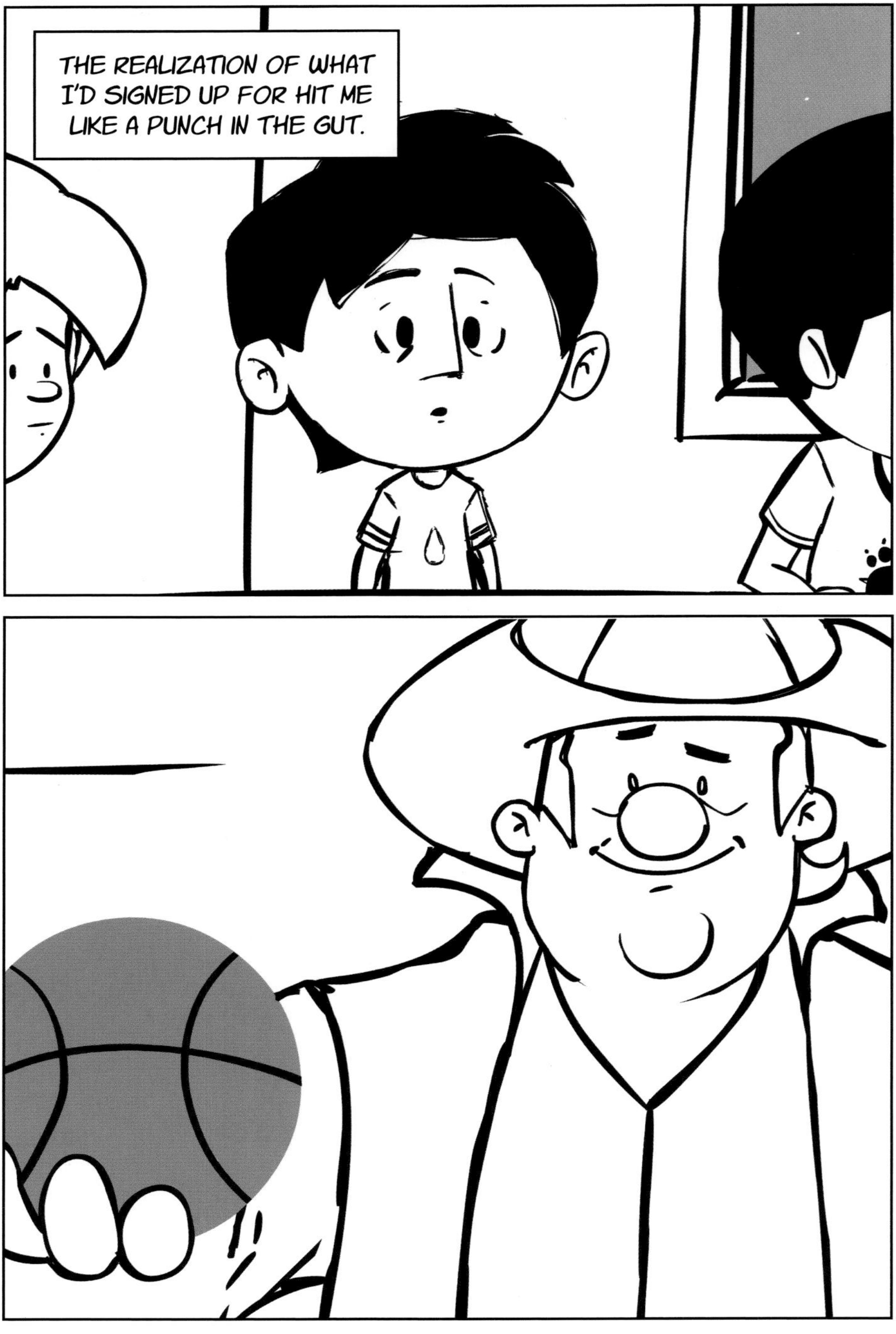
THE REALIZATION OF WHAT I'D SIGNED UP FOR HIT ME LIKE A PUNCH IN THE GUT.

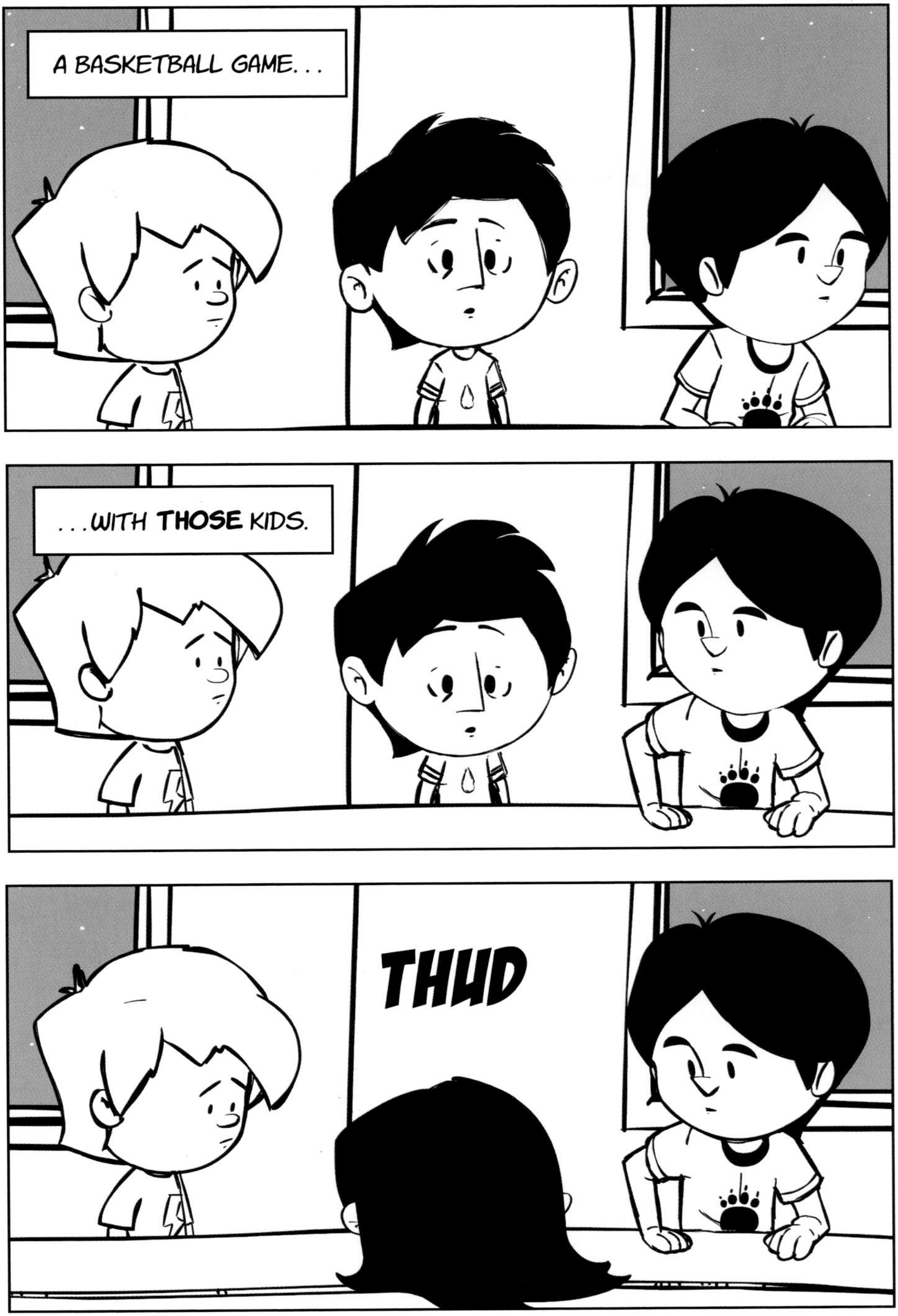
A BASKETBALL GAME...
...WITH THOSE KIDS.
THUD

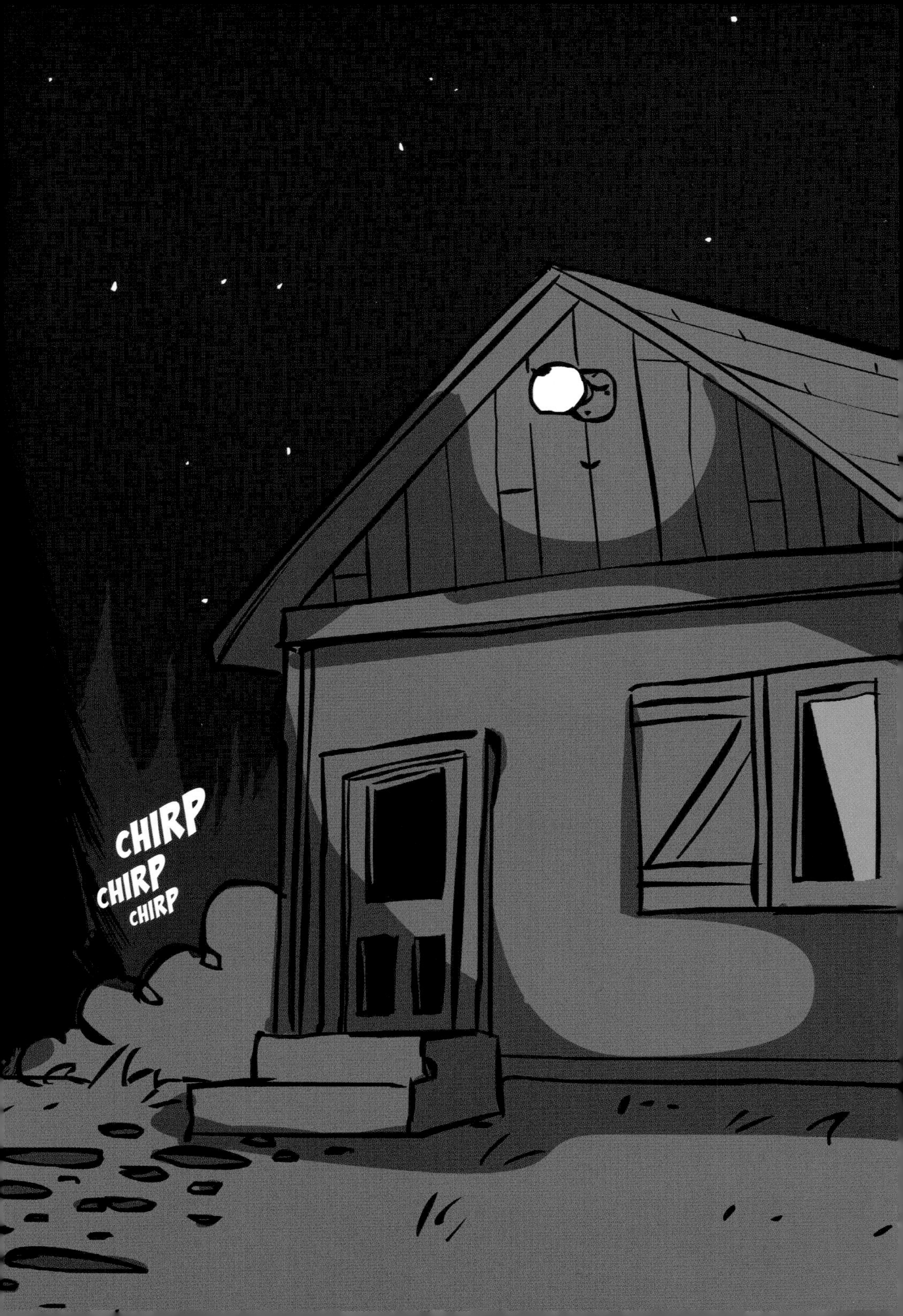
CHIRP
CHIRP
CHIRP

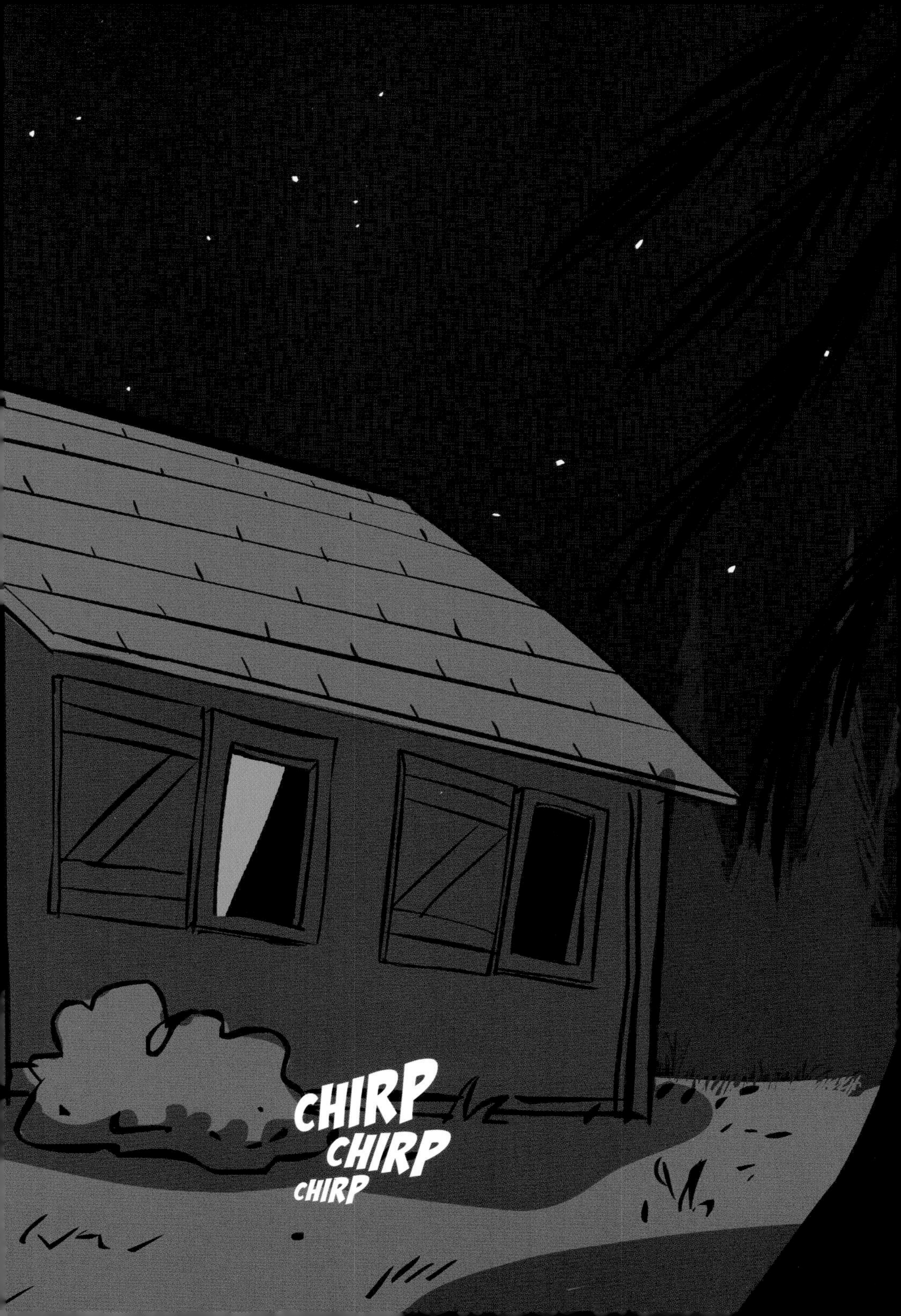
CHIRP
CHIRP
CHIRP

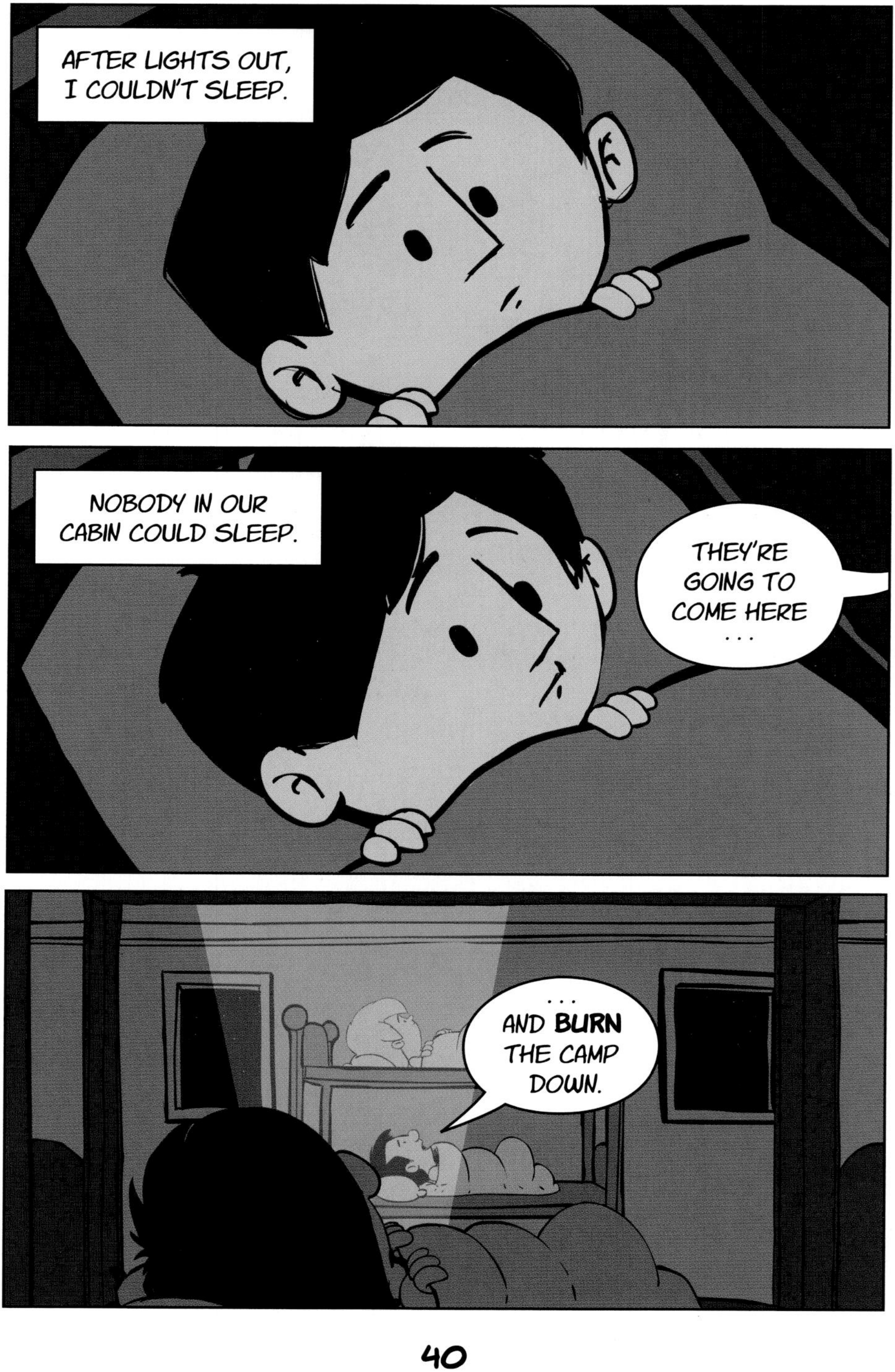
AFTER LIGHTS OUT, I COULDN'T SLEEP.
NOBODY IN OUR CABIN COULD SLEEP.
THEY'RE GOING TO COME HERE . . .
. . . AND **BURN** THE CAMP DOWN.

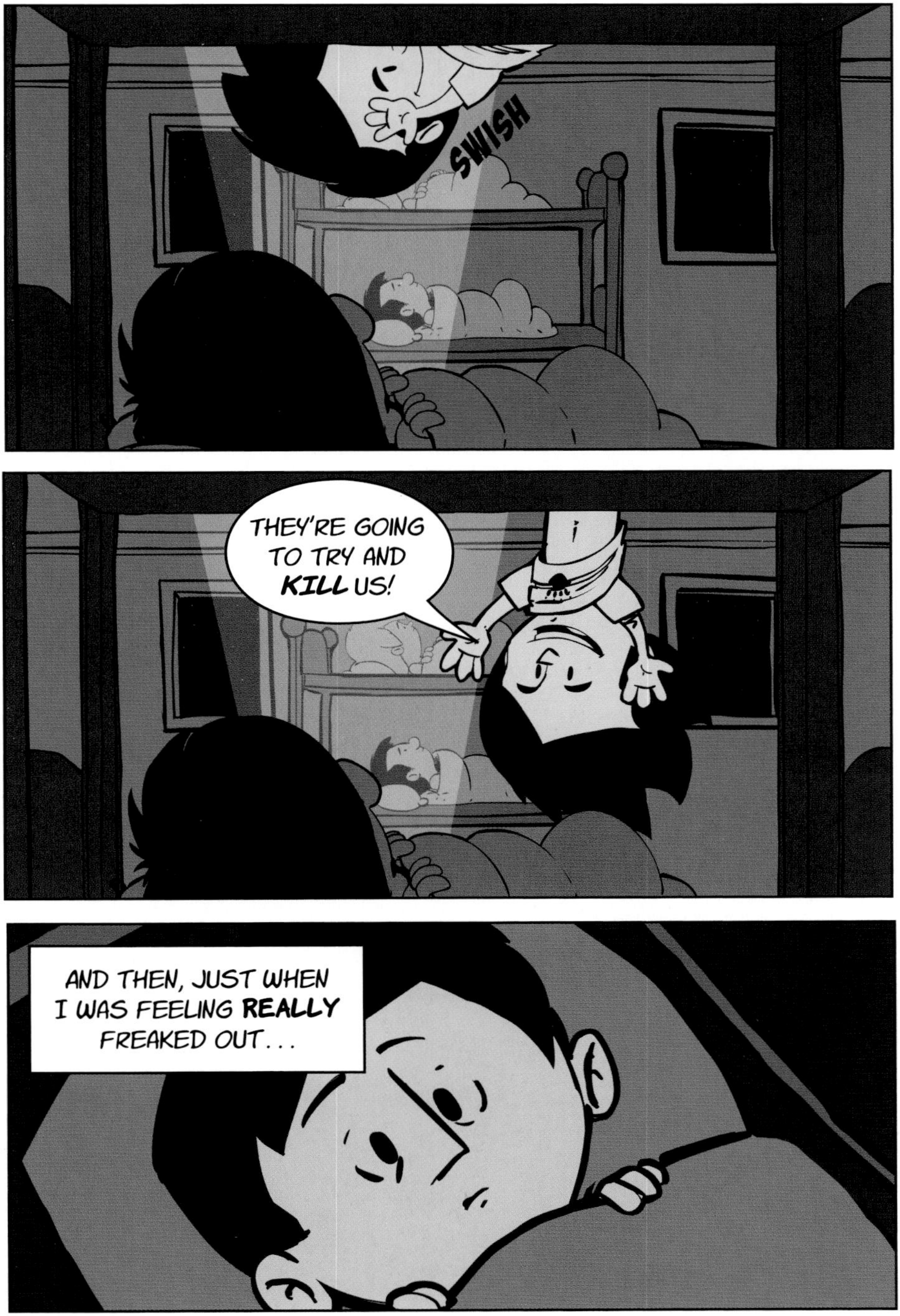
SWISH
THEY'RE GOING TO TRY AND **KILL** US!
AND THEN, JUST WHEN I WAS FEELING **REALLY** FREAKED OUT . . .

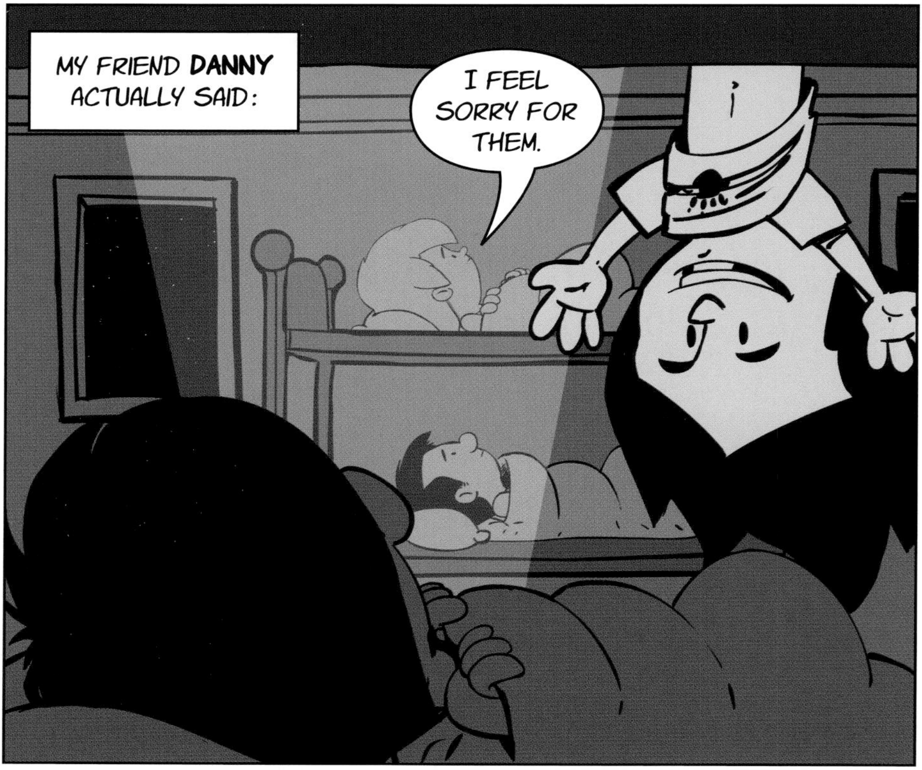
MY FRIEND **DANNY** ACTUALLY SAID:
I FEEL SORRY FOR THEM.

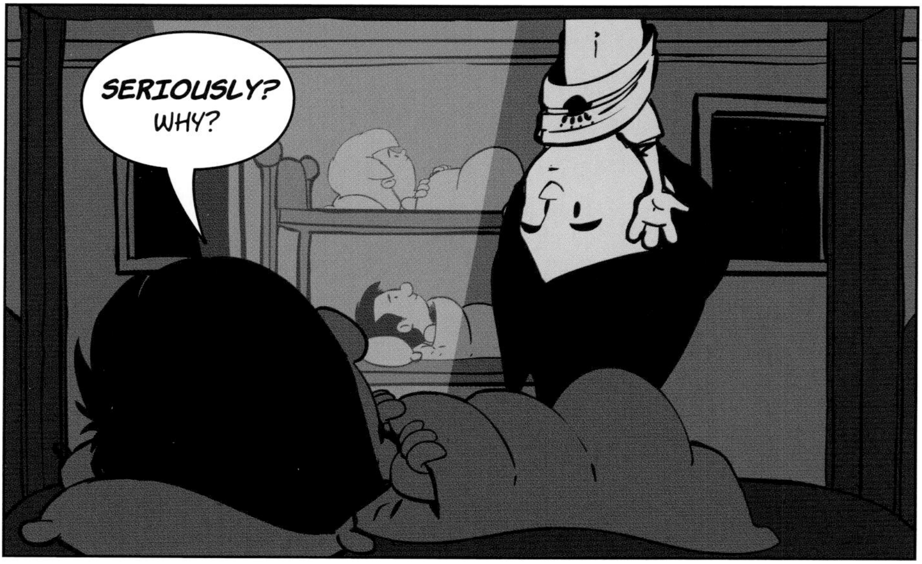
SERIOUSLY? WHY?

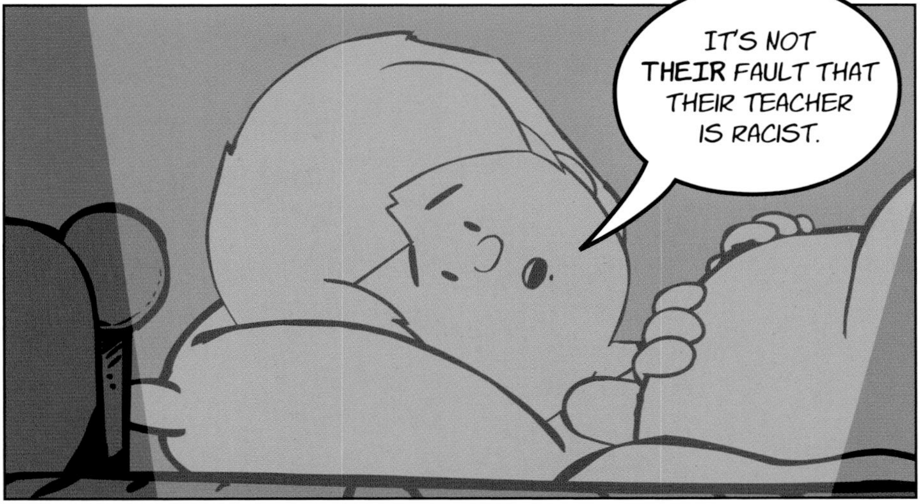
IT'S NOT **THEIR** FAULT THAT THEIR TEACHER IS RACIST.

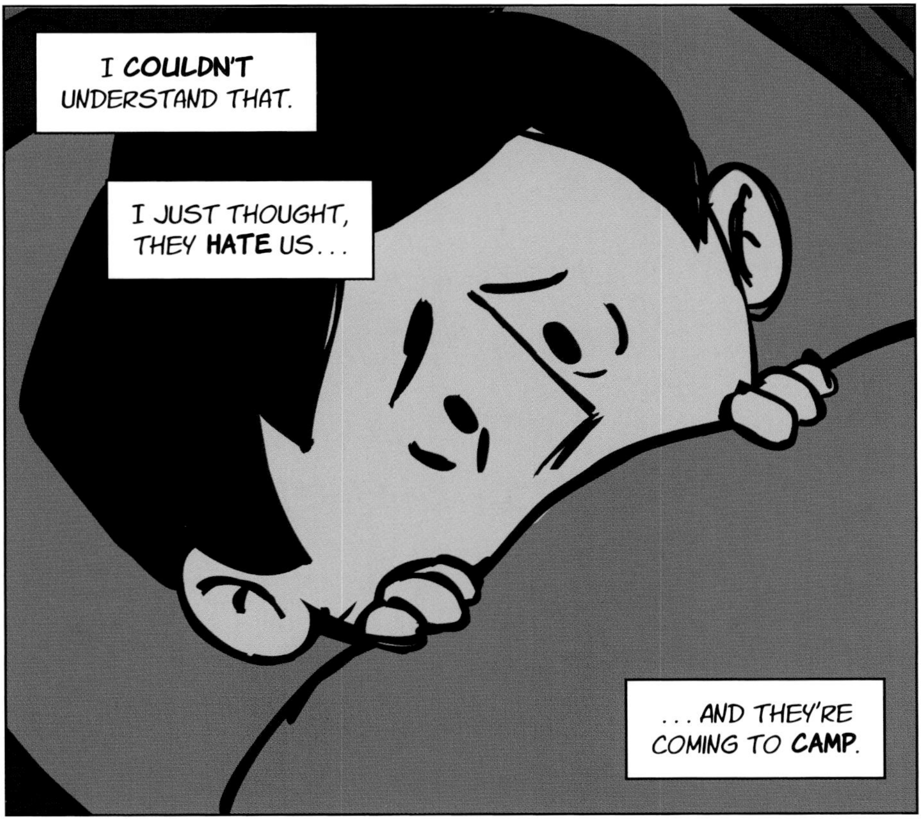
I **COULDN'T** UNDERSTAND THAT.
I JUST THOUGHT, THEY **HATE** US . . .
. . . AND THEY'RE COMING TO **CAMP**.

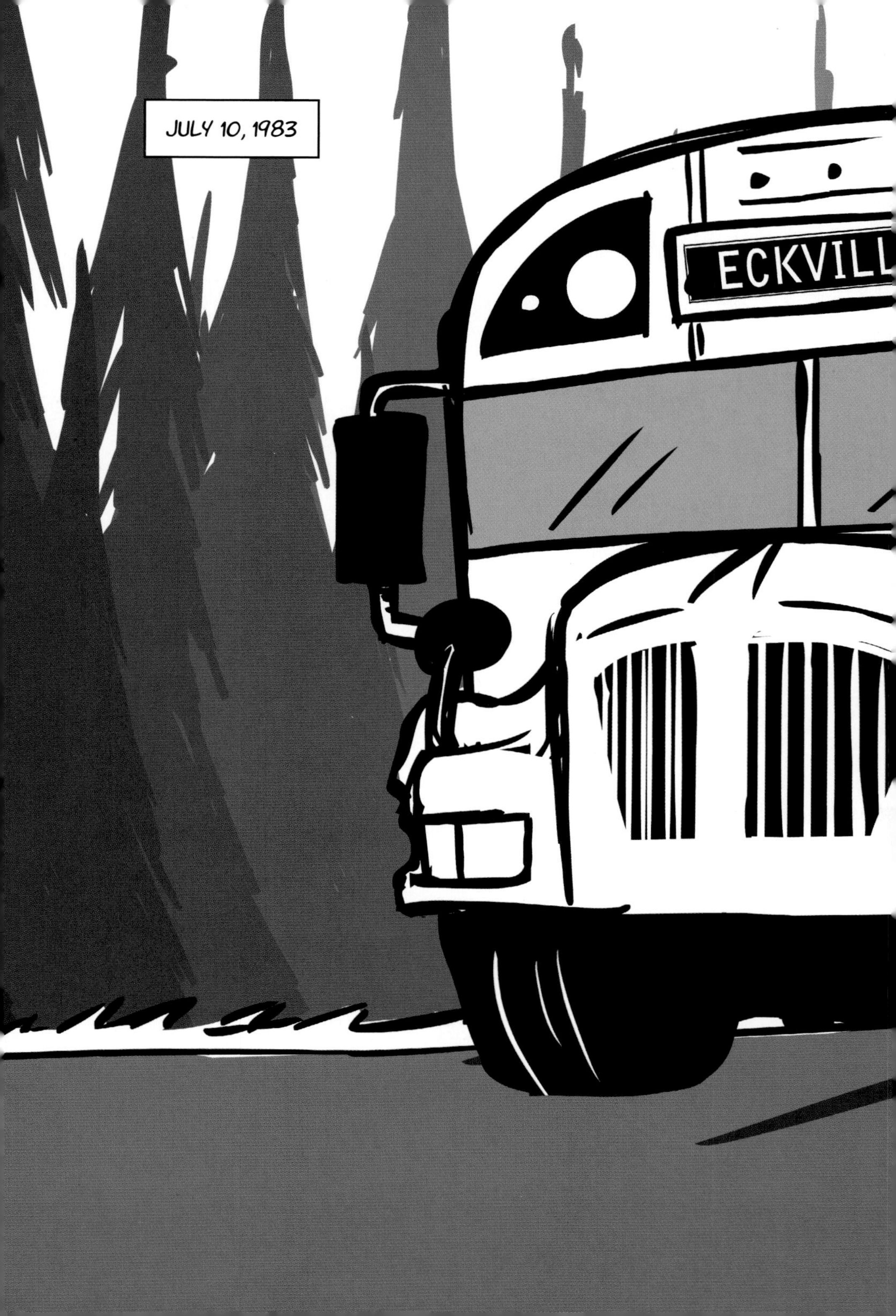
JULY 10, 1983
ECKVILL

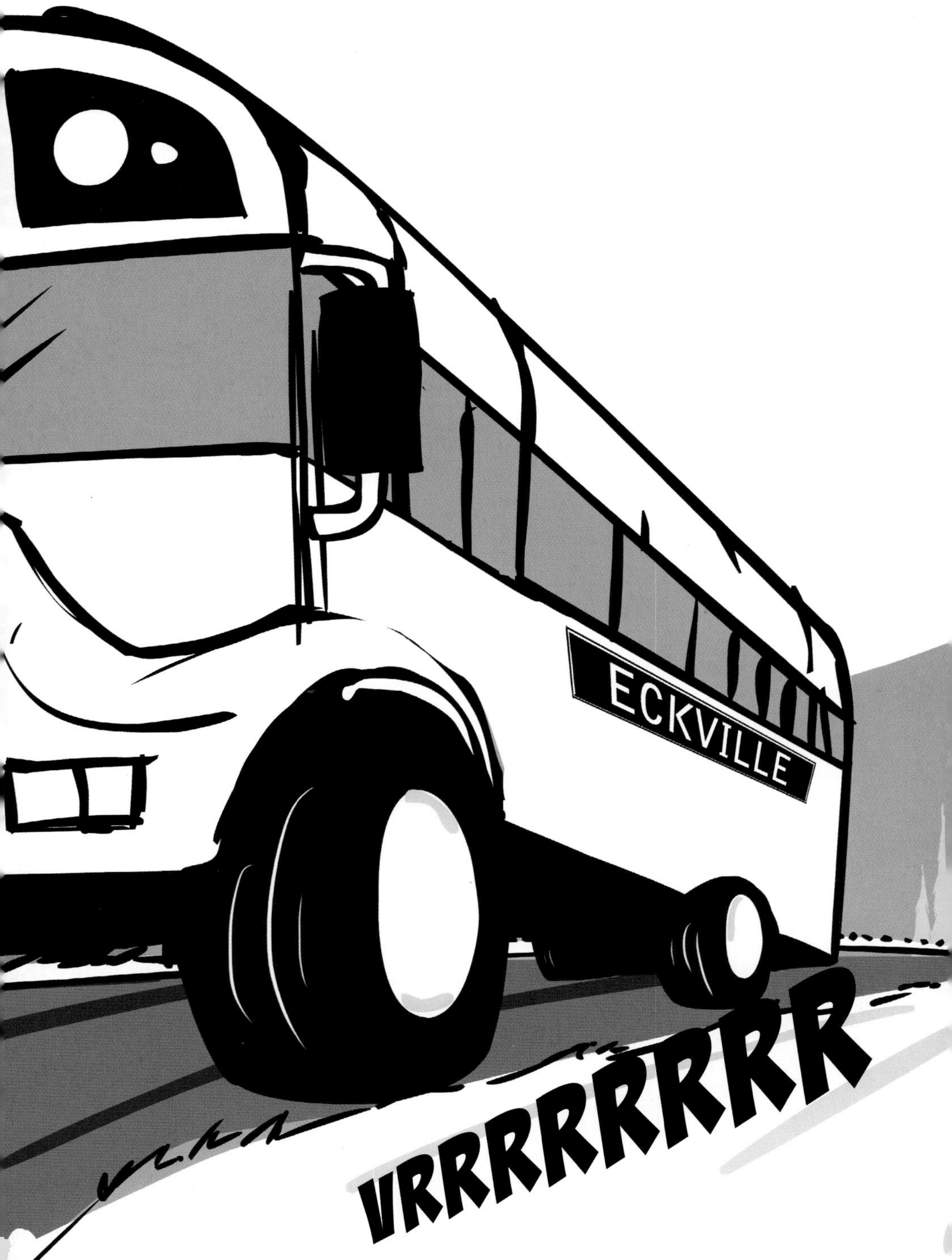
ECKVILLE
VRRRRRRRRR

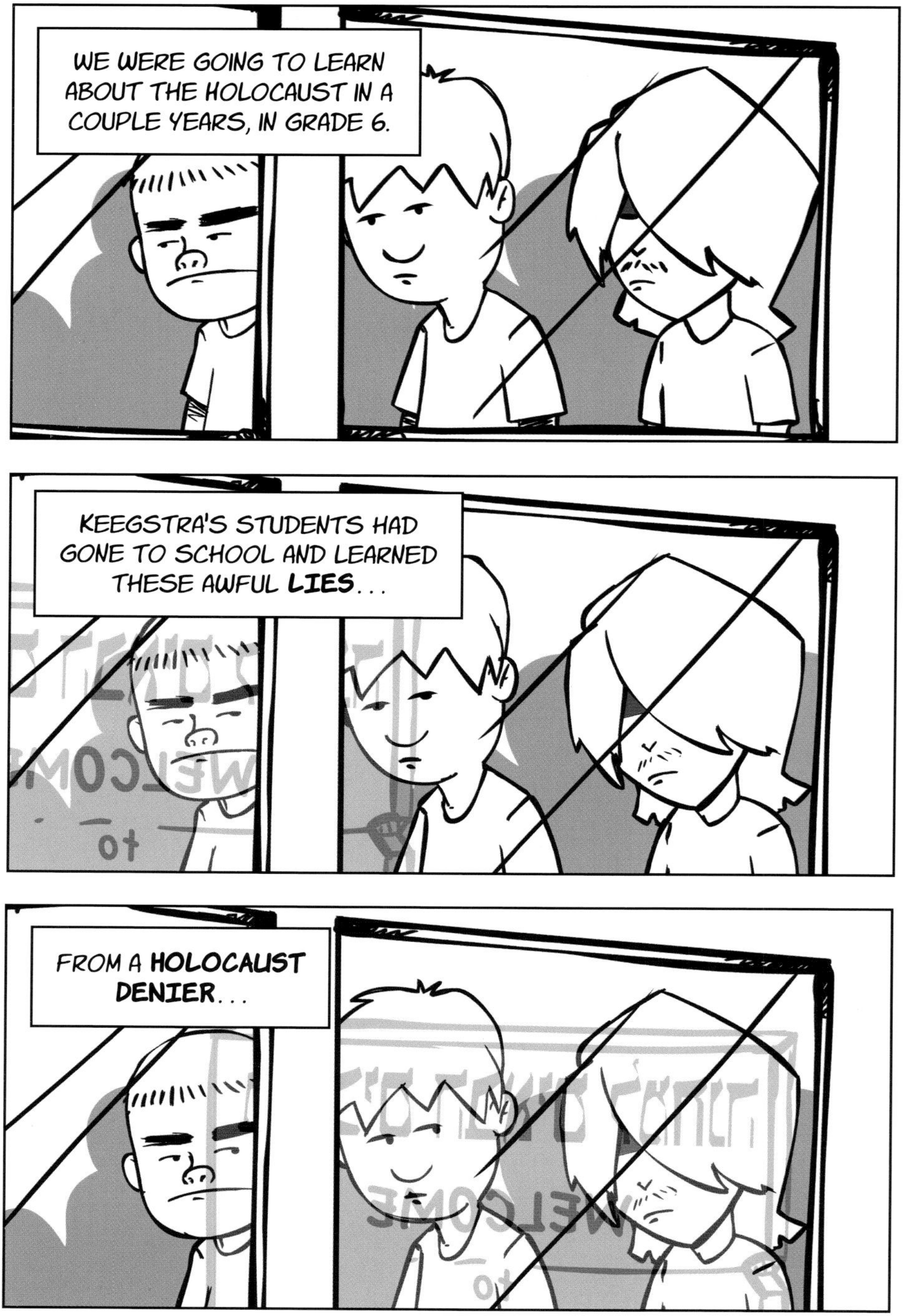
WE WERE GOING TO LEARN ABOUT THE HOLOCAUST IN A COUPLE YEARS, IN GRADE 6.
KEEGSTRA'S STUDENTS HAD GONE TO SCHOOL AND LEARNED THESE AWFUL LIES...
FROM A HOLOCAUST DENIER...

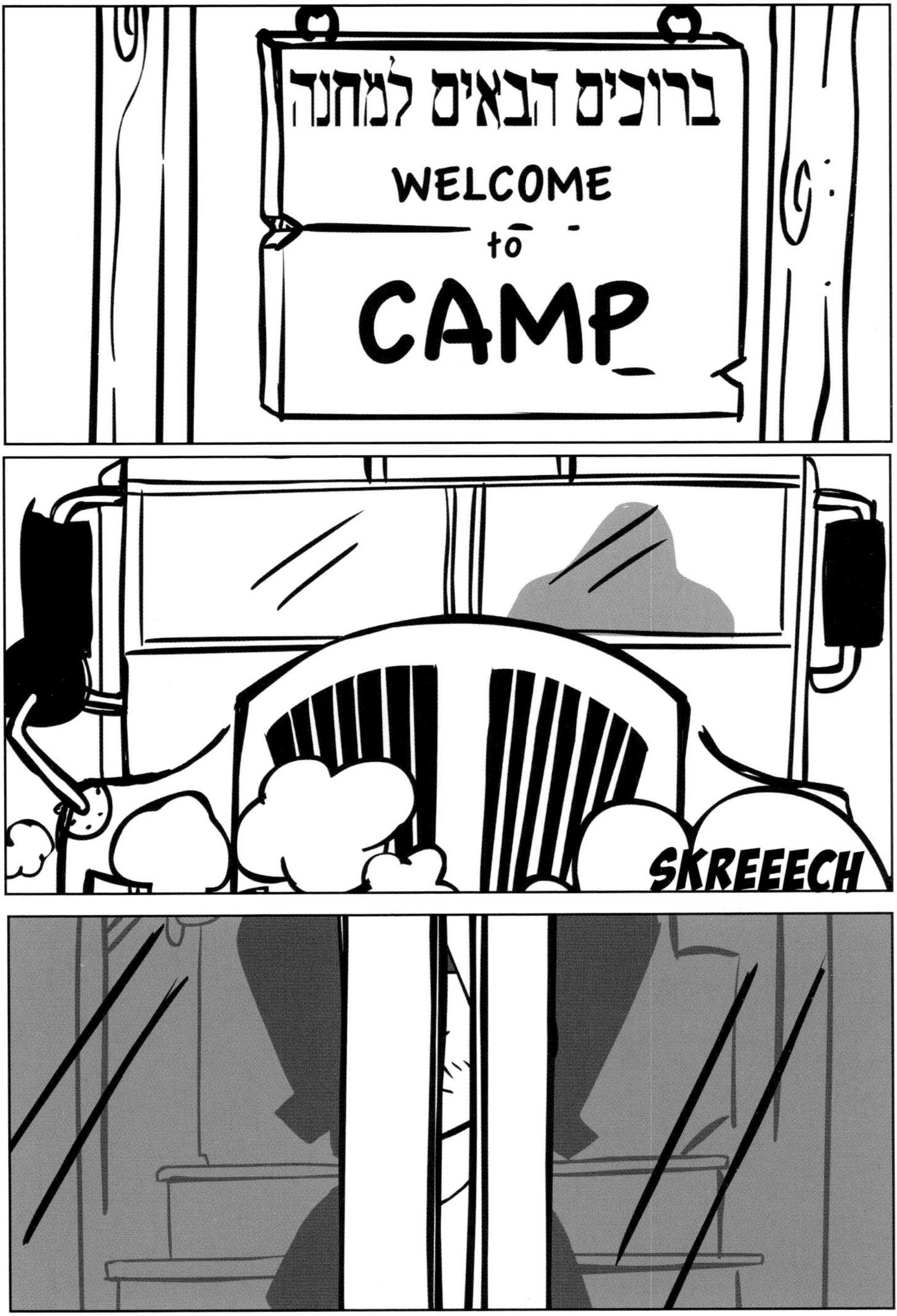
ברוכים הבאים למחנה
WELCOME
to
CAMP
SKREEECH

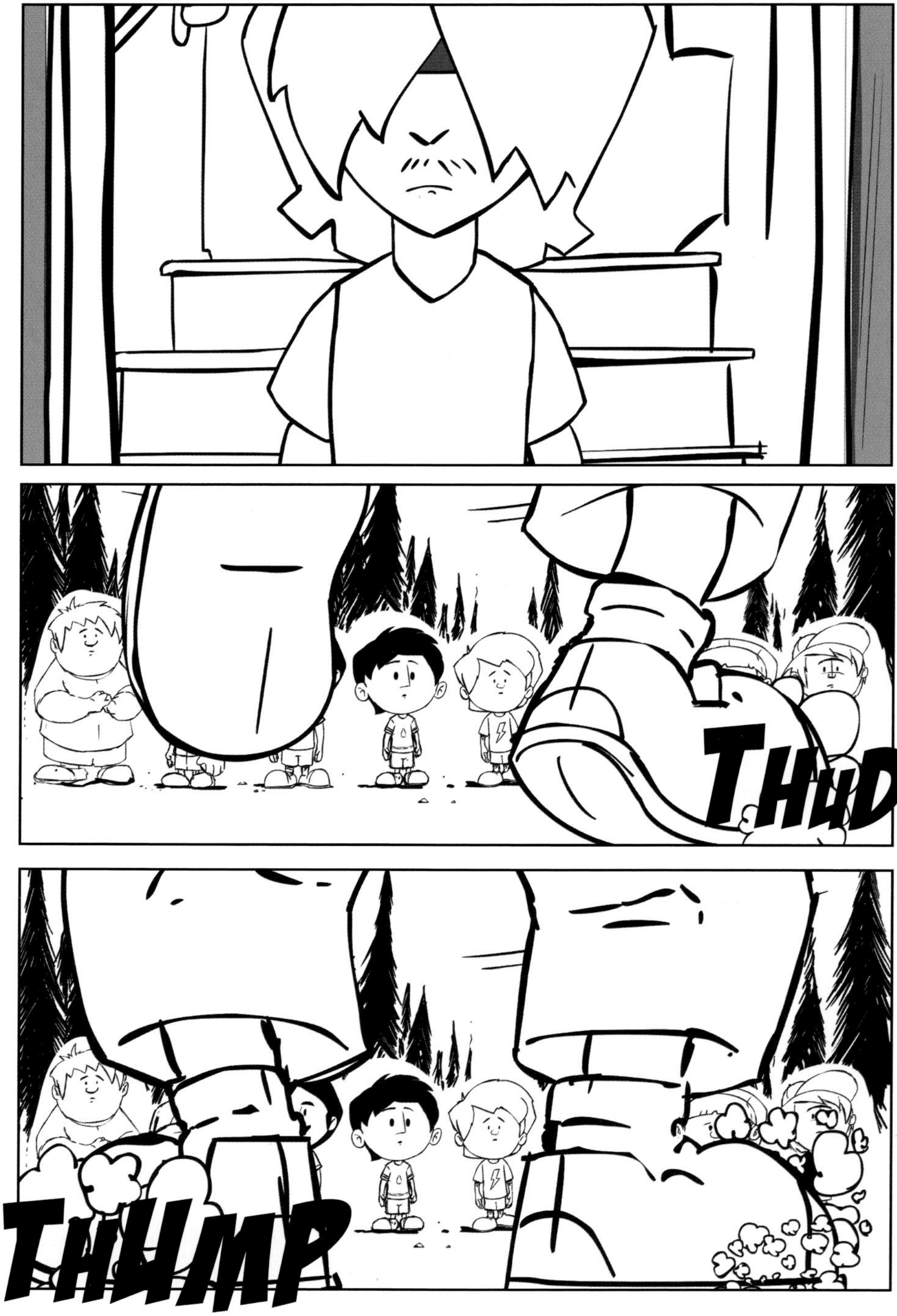
THUD
THUMP

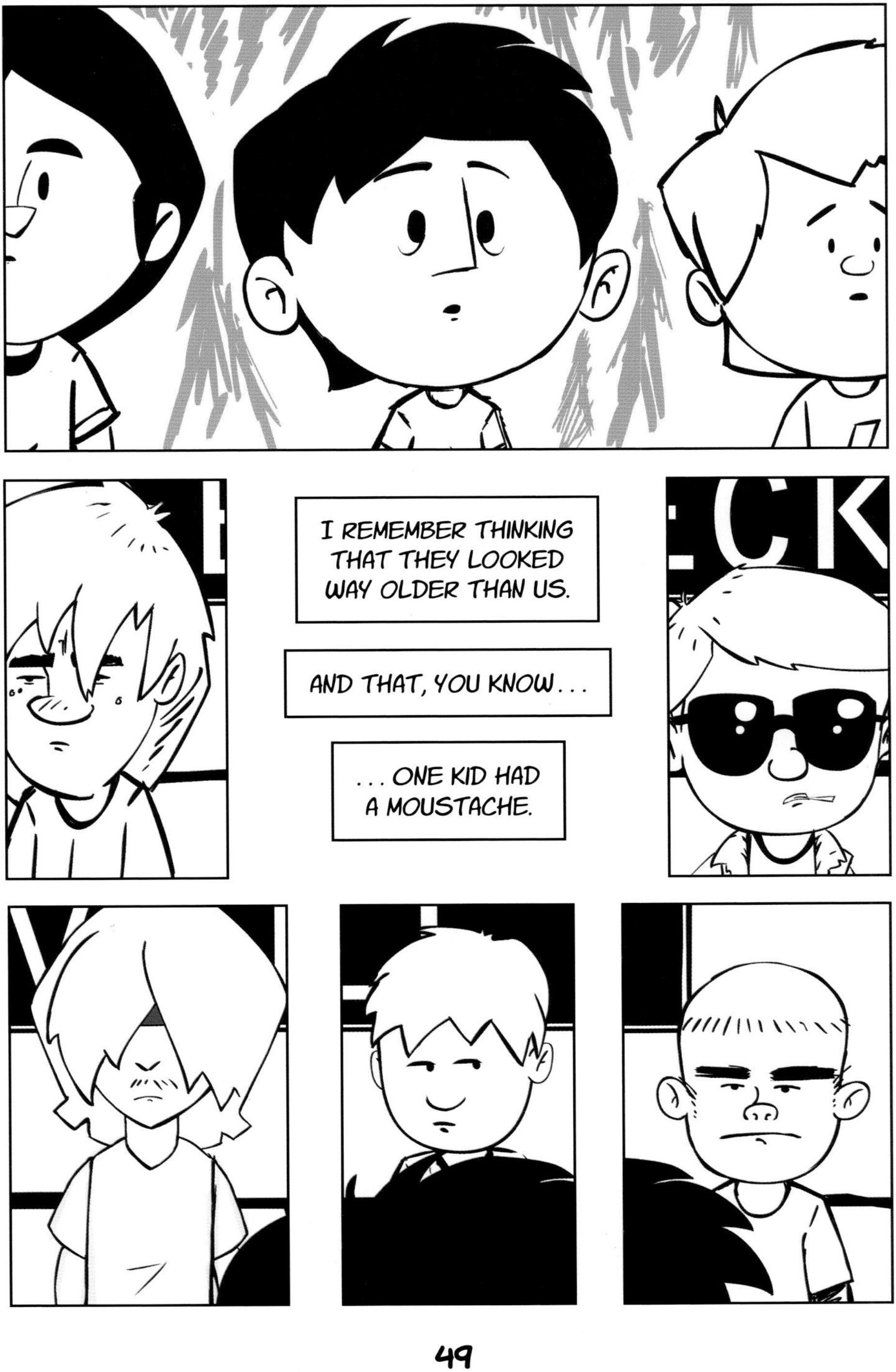
I REMEMBER THINKING THAT THEY LOOKED WAY OLDER THAN US.
AND THAT, YOU KNOW...
...ONE KID HAD A MOUSTACHE.

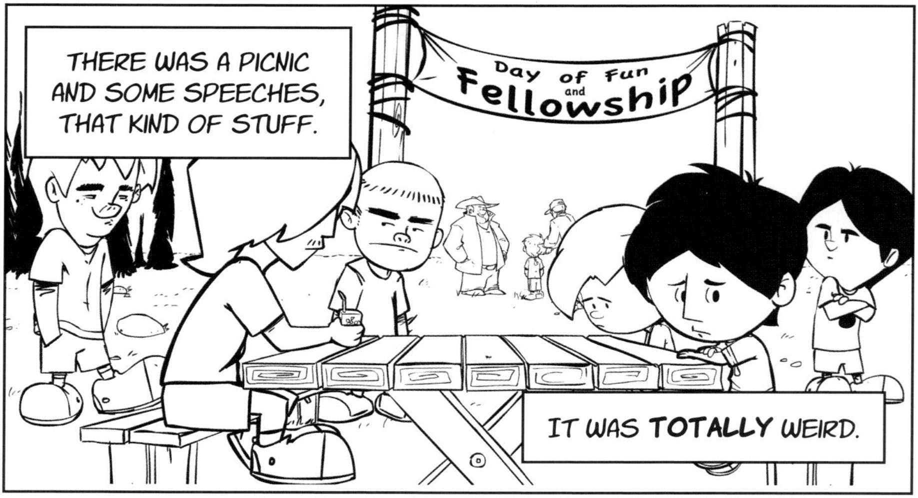
THERE WAS A PICNIC AND SOME SPEECHES, THAT KIND OF STUFF.
Day of Fun and Fellowship
IT WAS **TOTALLY** WEIRD.

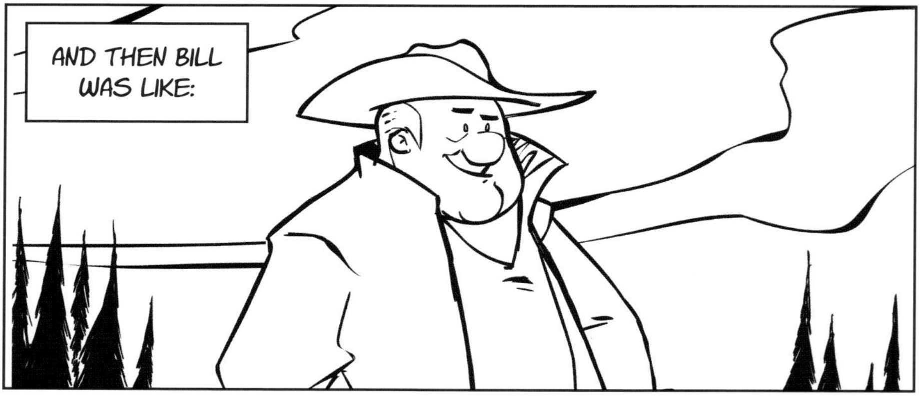
AND THEN BILL WAS LIKE:

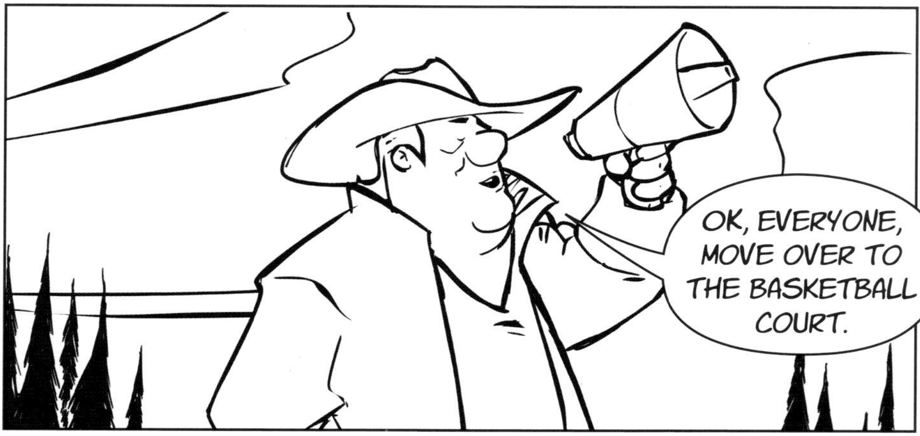
OK, EVERYONE, MOVE OVER TO THE BASKETBALL COURT.

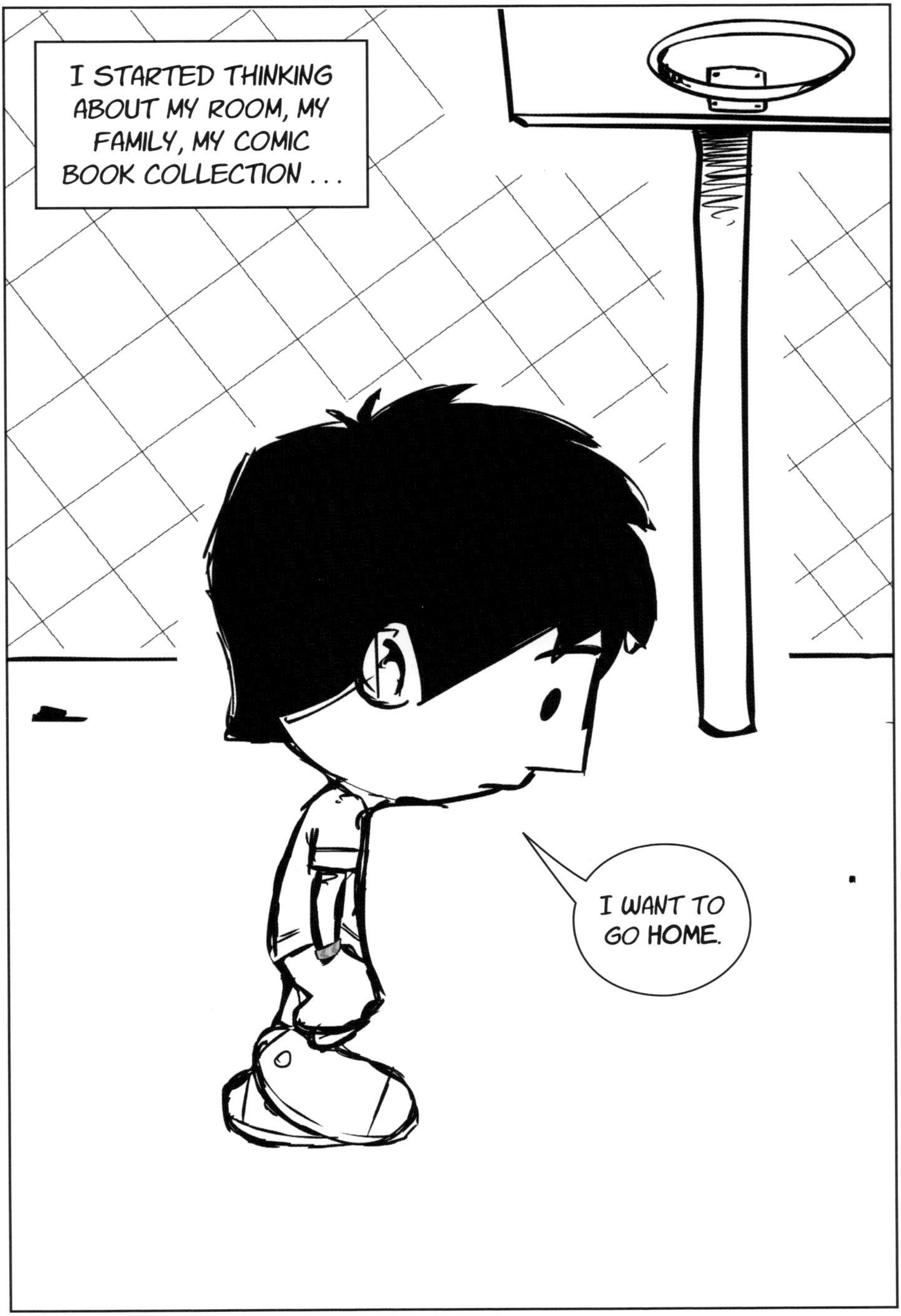
I STARTED THINKING ABOUT MY ROOM, MY FAMILY, MY COMIC BOOK COLLECTION . . .
I WANT TO GO HOME.

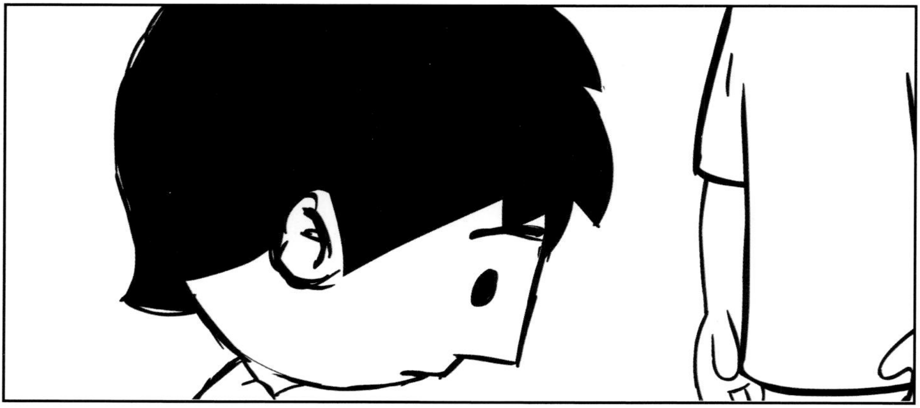
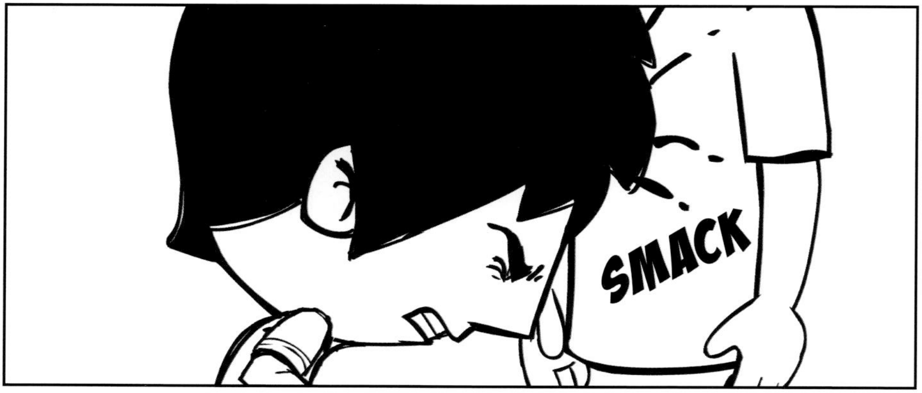
SMACK
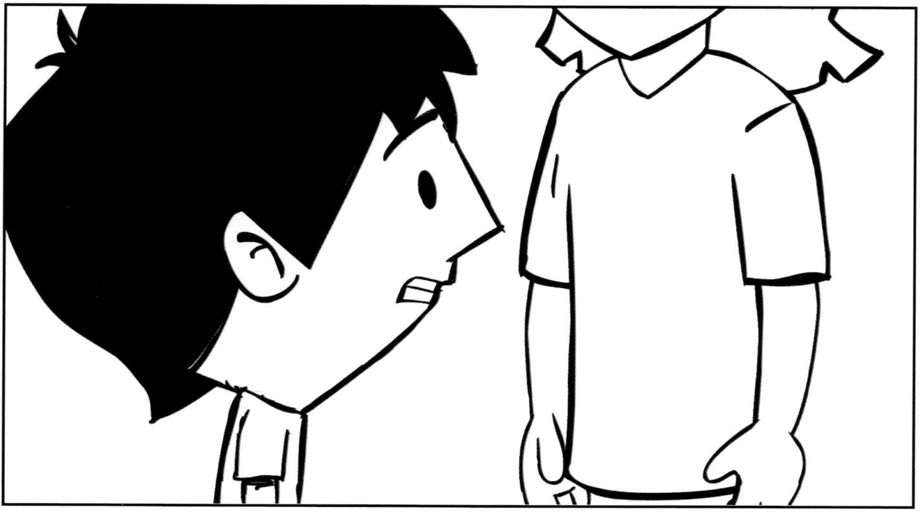

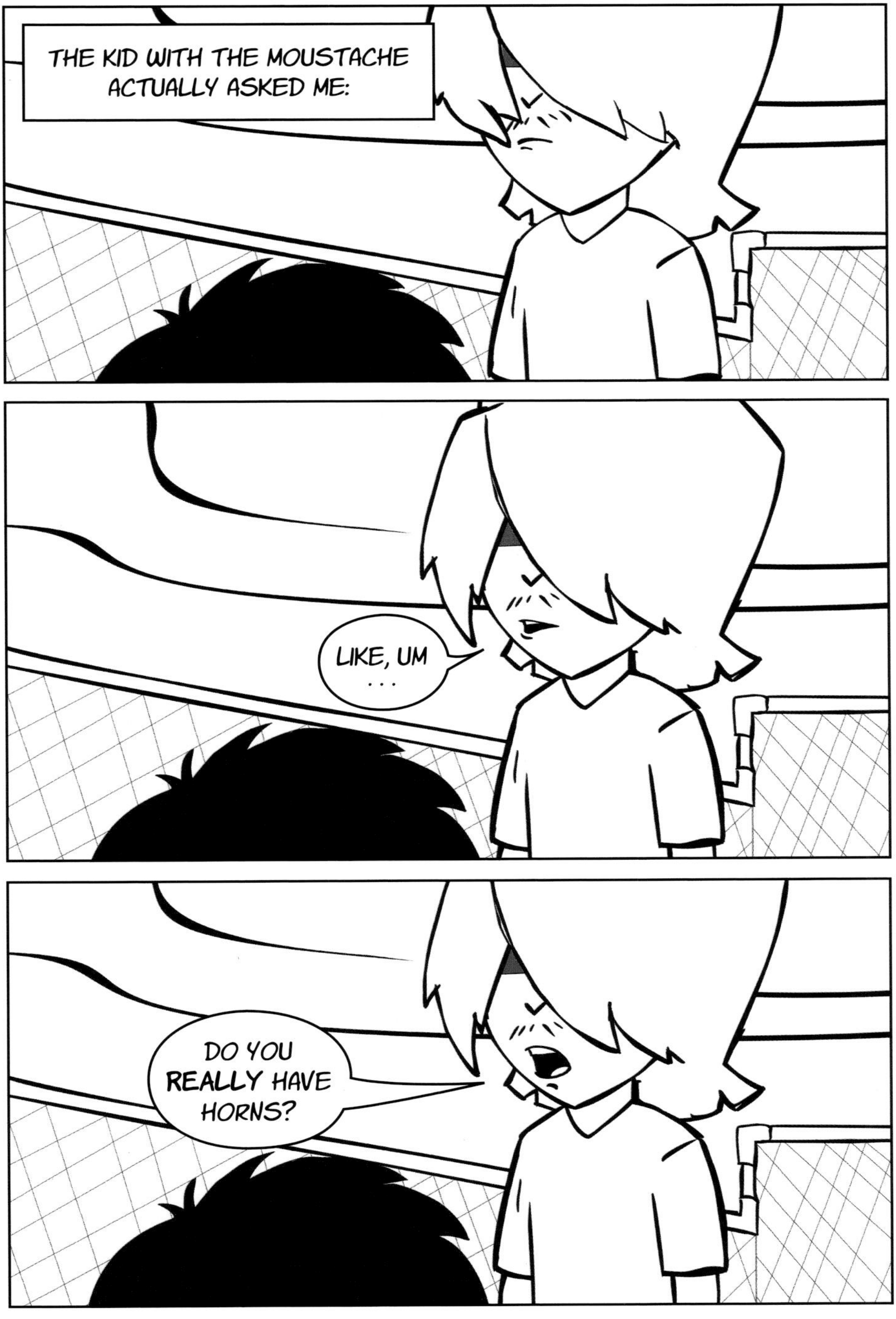
THE KID WITH THE MOUSTACHE ACTUALLY ASKED ME:
LIKE, UM . . .
DO YOU **REALLY** HAVE HORNS?

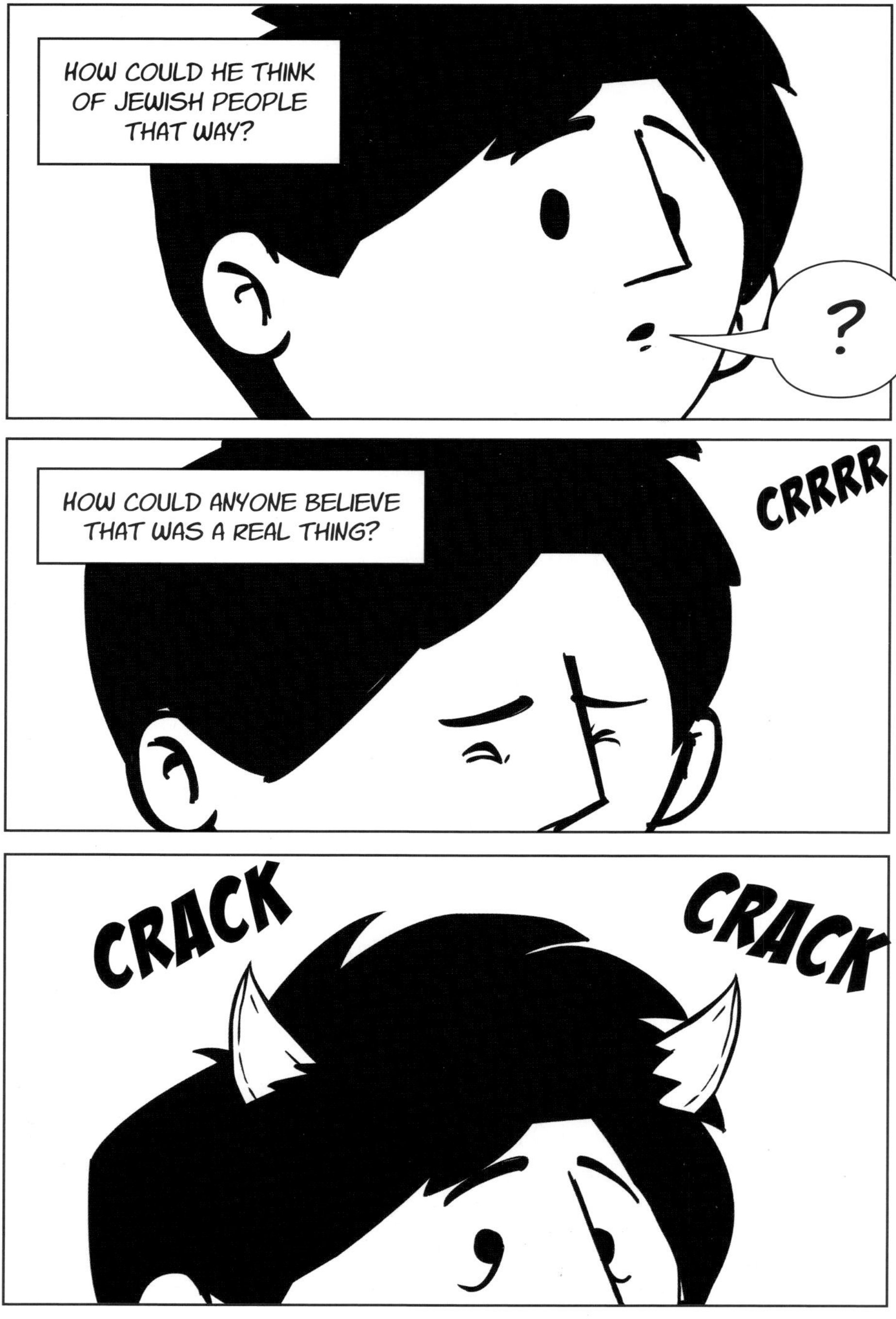
HOW COULD HE THINK OF JEWISH PEOPLE THAT WAY?
?
HOW COULD ANYONE BELIEVE THAT WAS A REAL THING?
CRRRR
CRACK
CRACK

IT WAS HUMILIATING.

I FELT ALONE —

THUMP

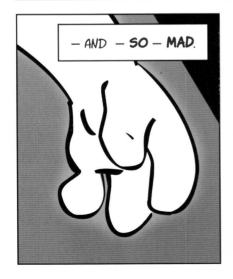

— AND — SO — MAD.

CRACK

55

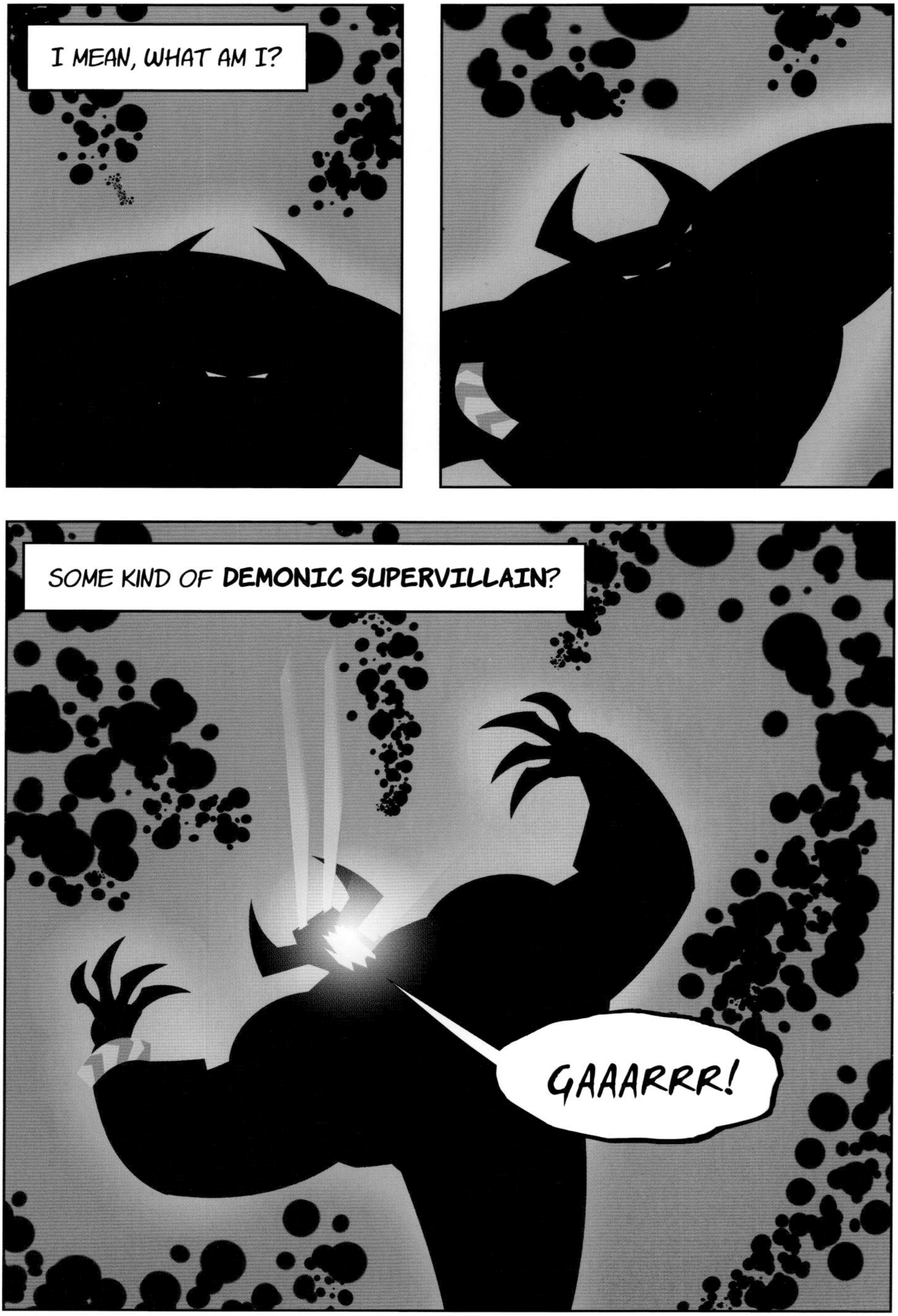
I MEAN, WHAT AM I?
SOME KIND OF DEMONIC SUPERVILLAIN?
GAAARRR!

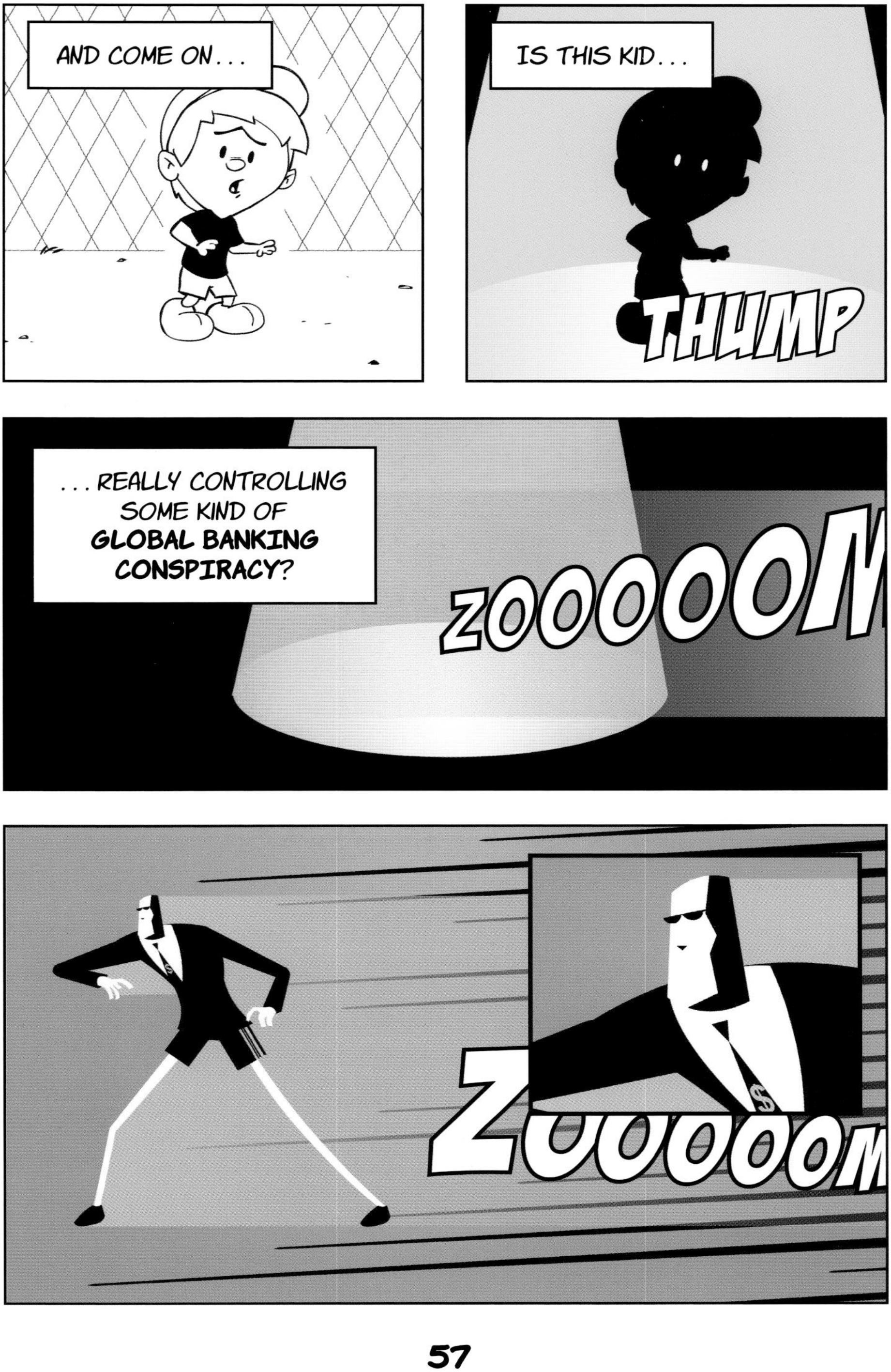
AND COME ON . . .
IS THIS KID . . .
THUMP
. . . REALLY CONTROLLING SOME KIND OF GLOBAL BANKING CONSPIRACY?
ZOOOOOOM
ZOOOOOOM

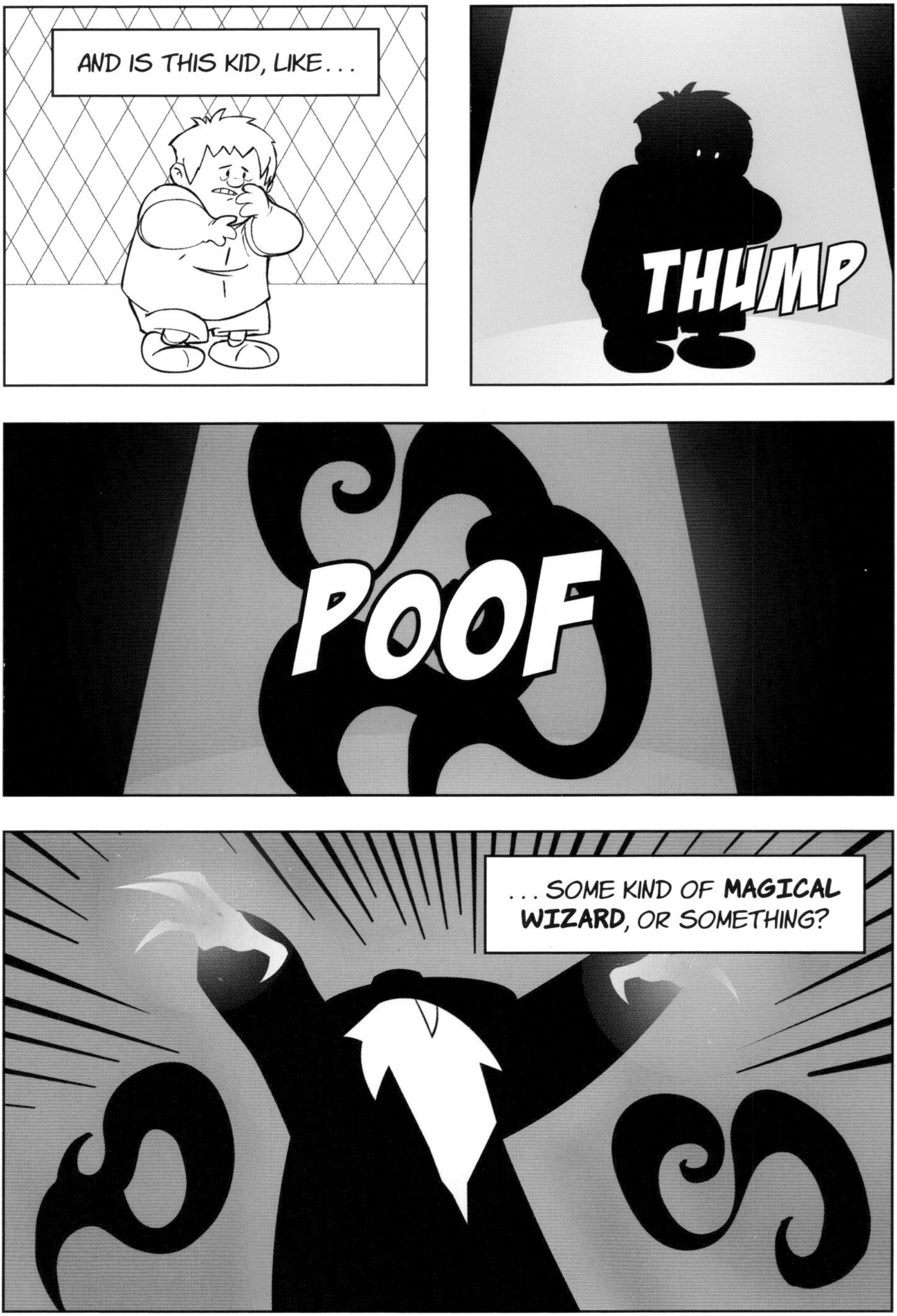
AND IS THIS KID, LIKE . . .
THUMP
POOF
. . . SOME KIND OF **MAGICAL WIZARD**, OR SOMETHING?

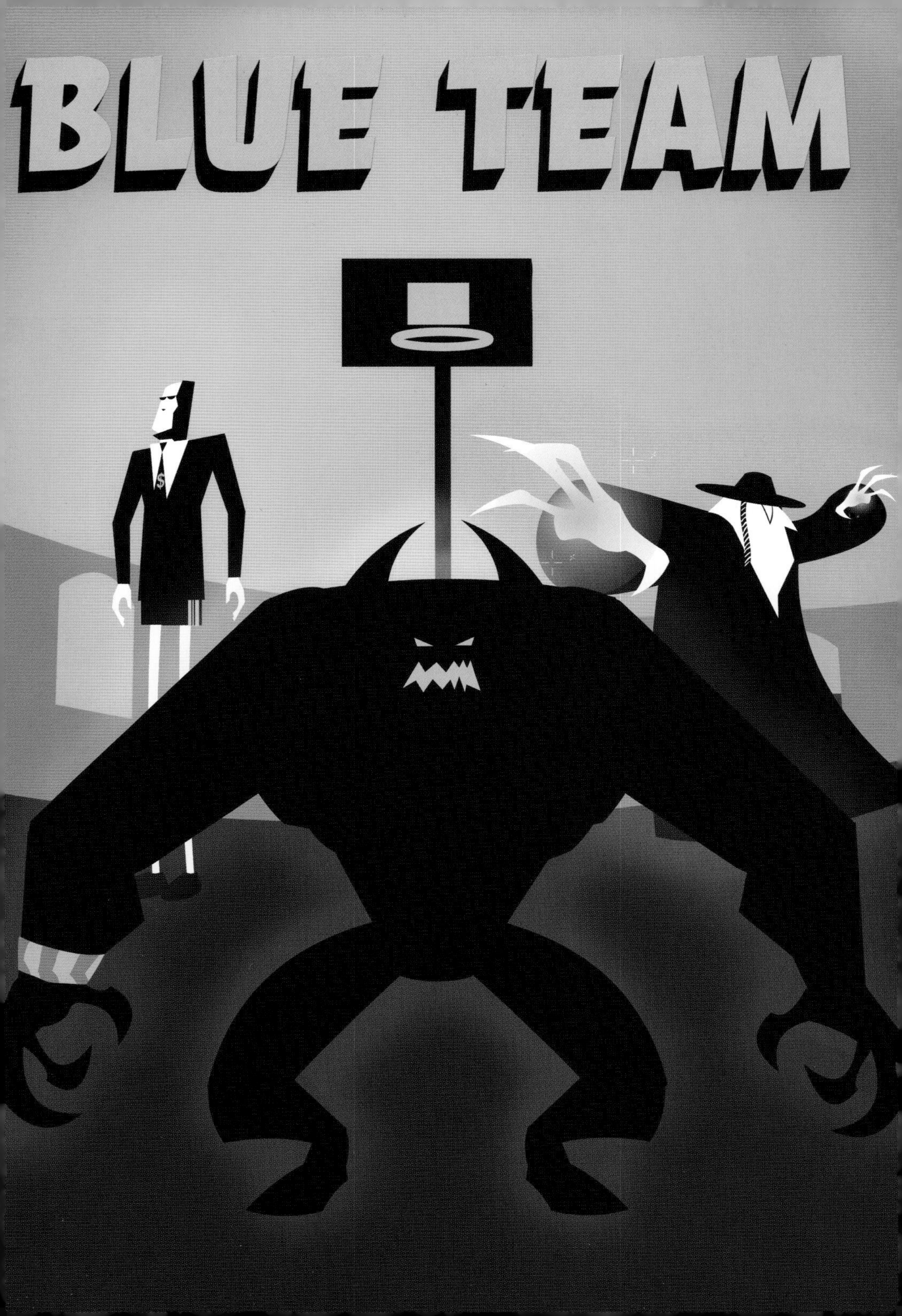
BLUE TEAM

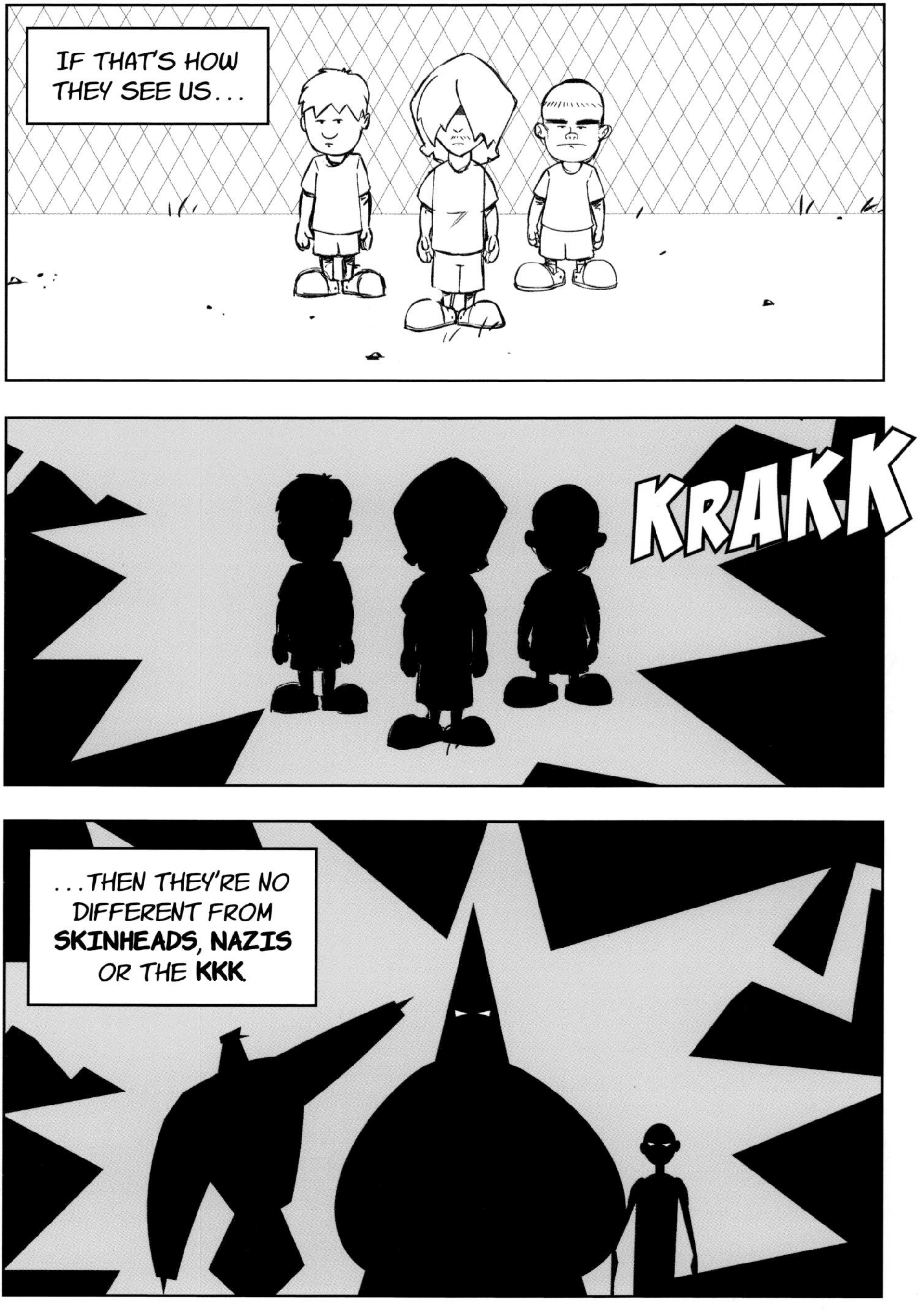
IF THAT'S HOW THEY SEE US . . .
KRAKK
. . . THEN THEY'RE NO DIFFERENT FROM **SKINHEADS**, **NAZIS** OR THE **KKK**.

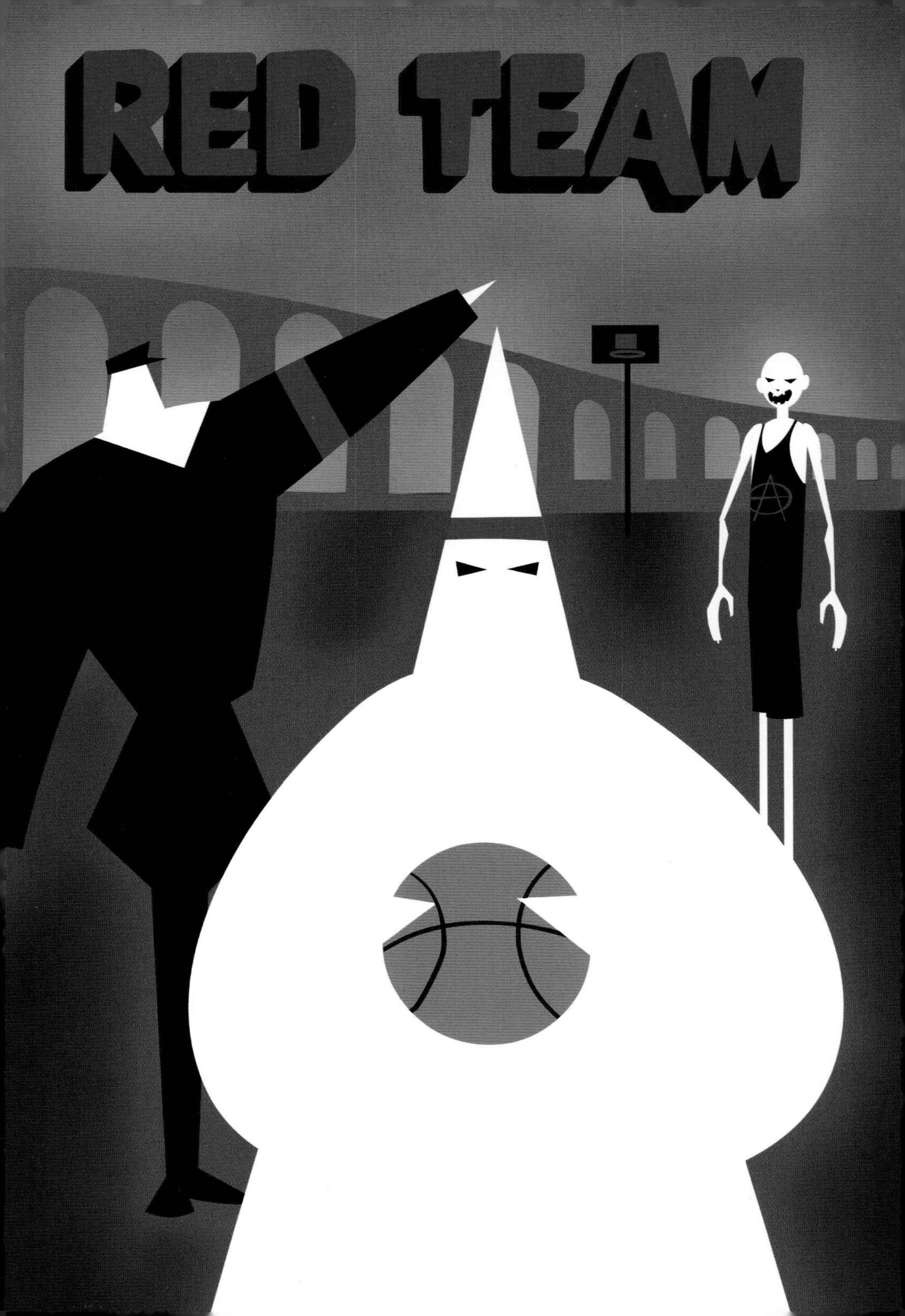
RED TEAM

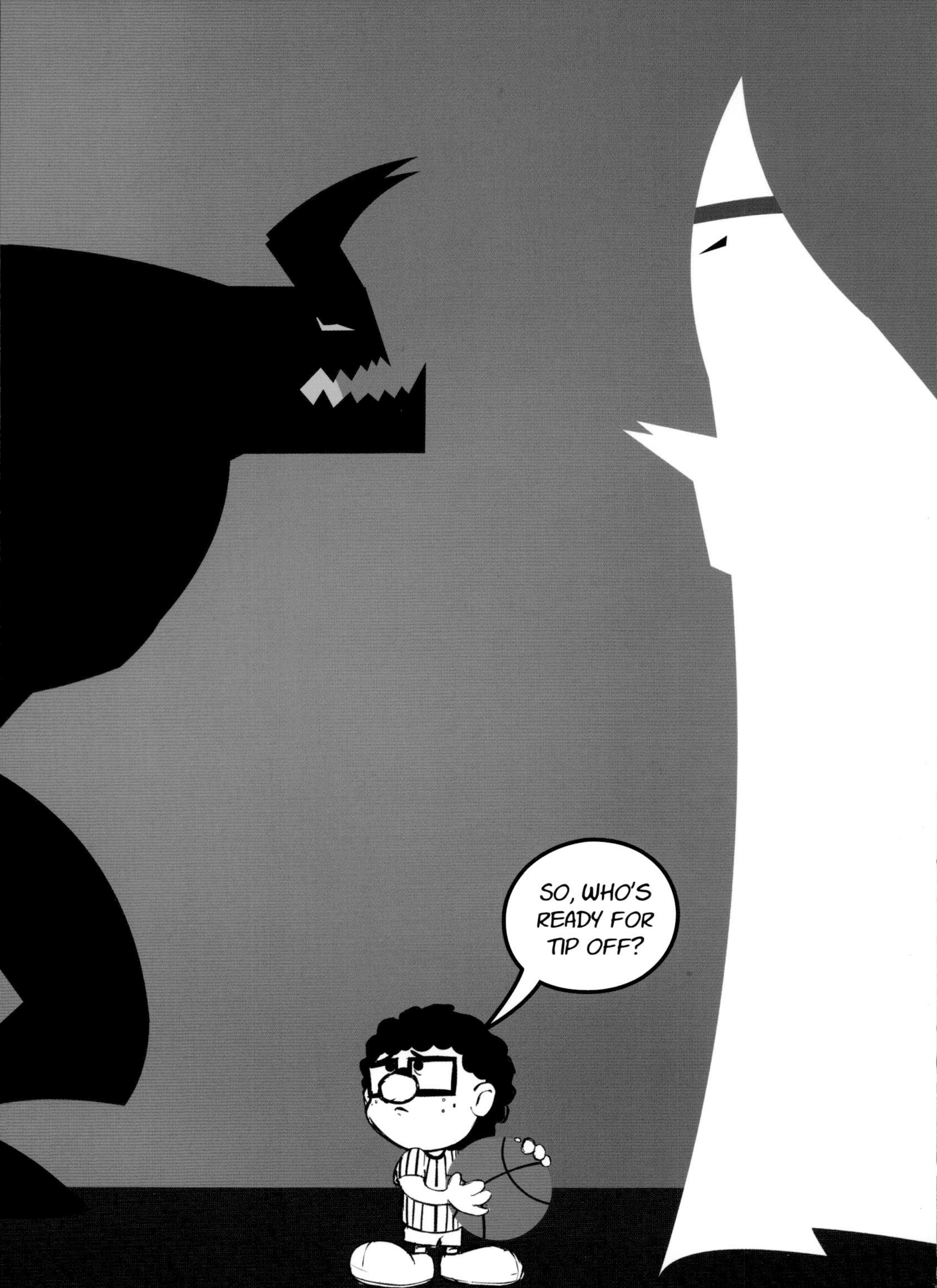
SO, WHO'S READY FOR TIP OFF?

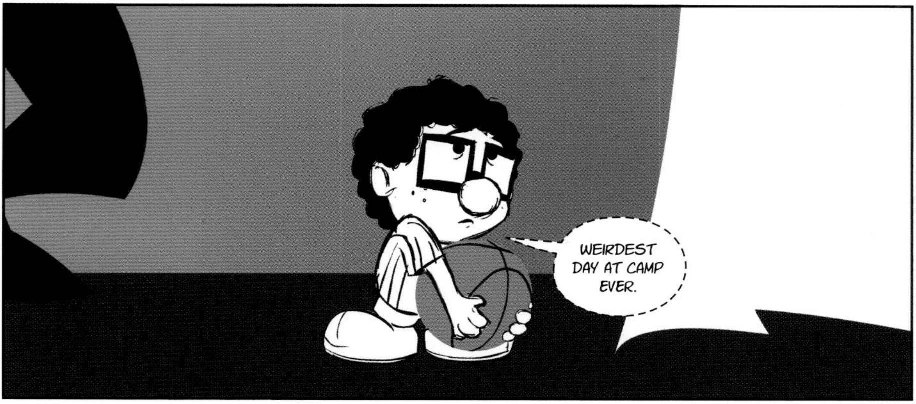
WEIRDEST DAY AT CAMP EVER.

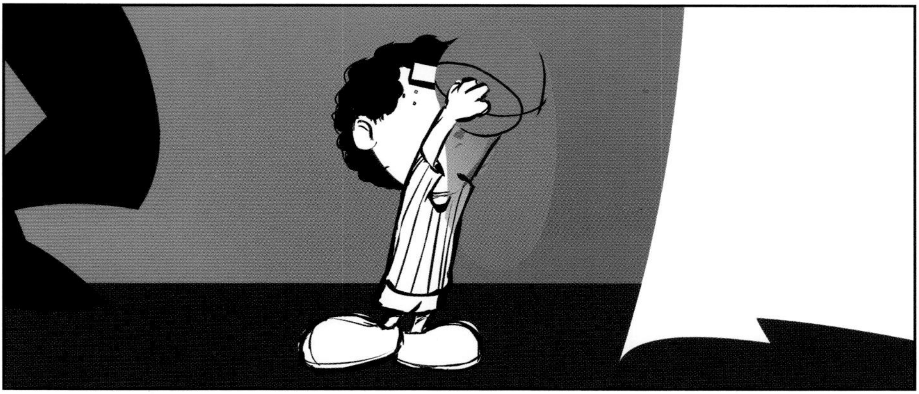

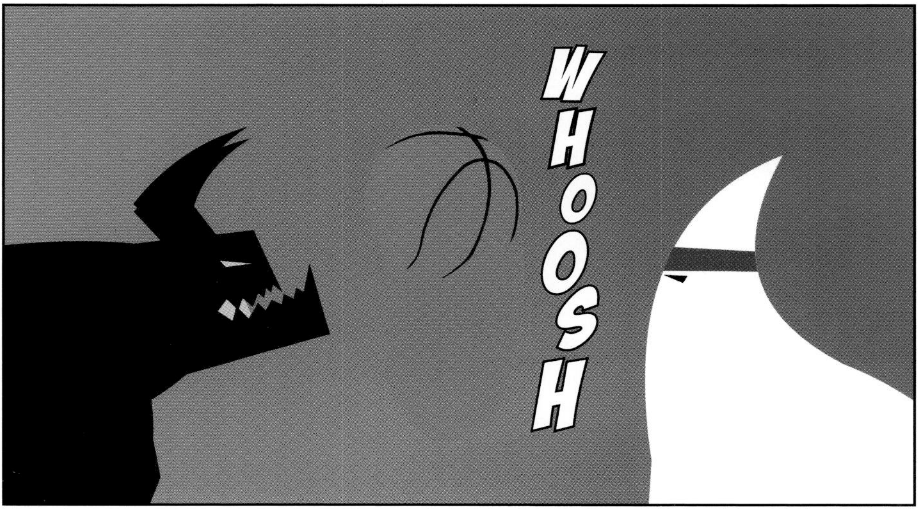
WHOOSH

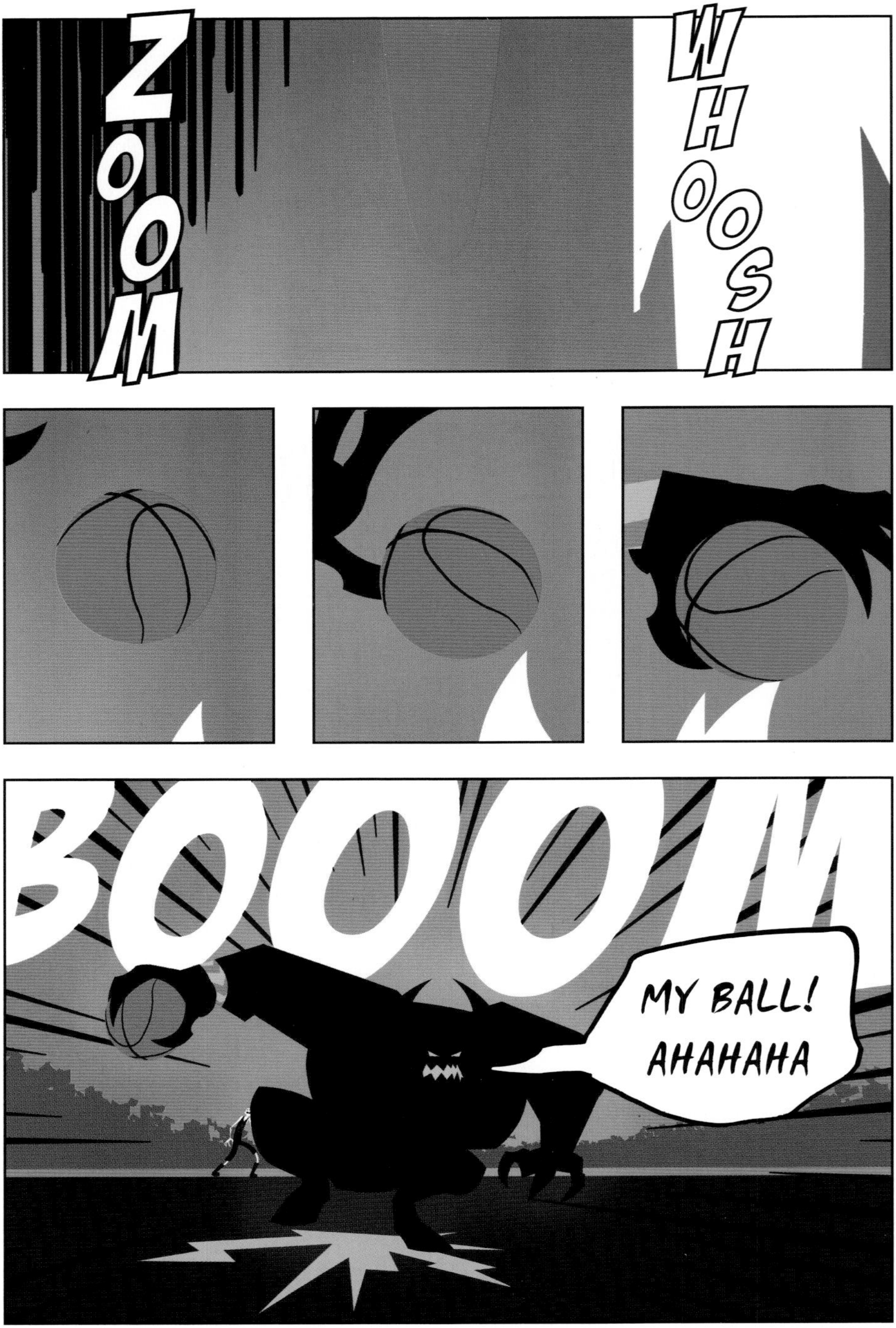
ZOOM
WHOOSH
BOOOM
MY BALL! AHAHAHA

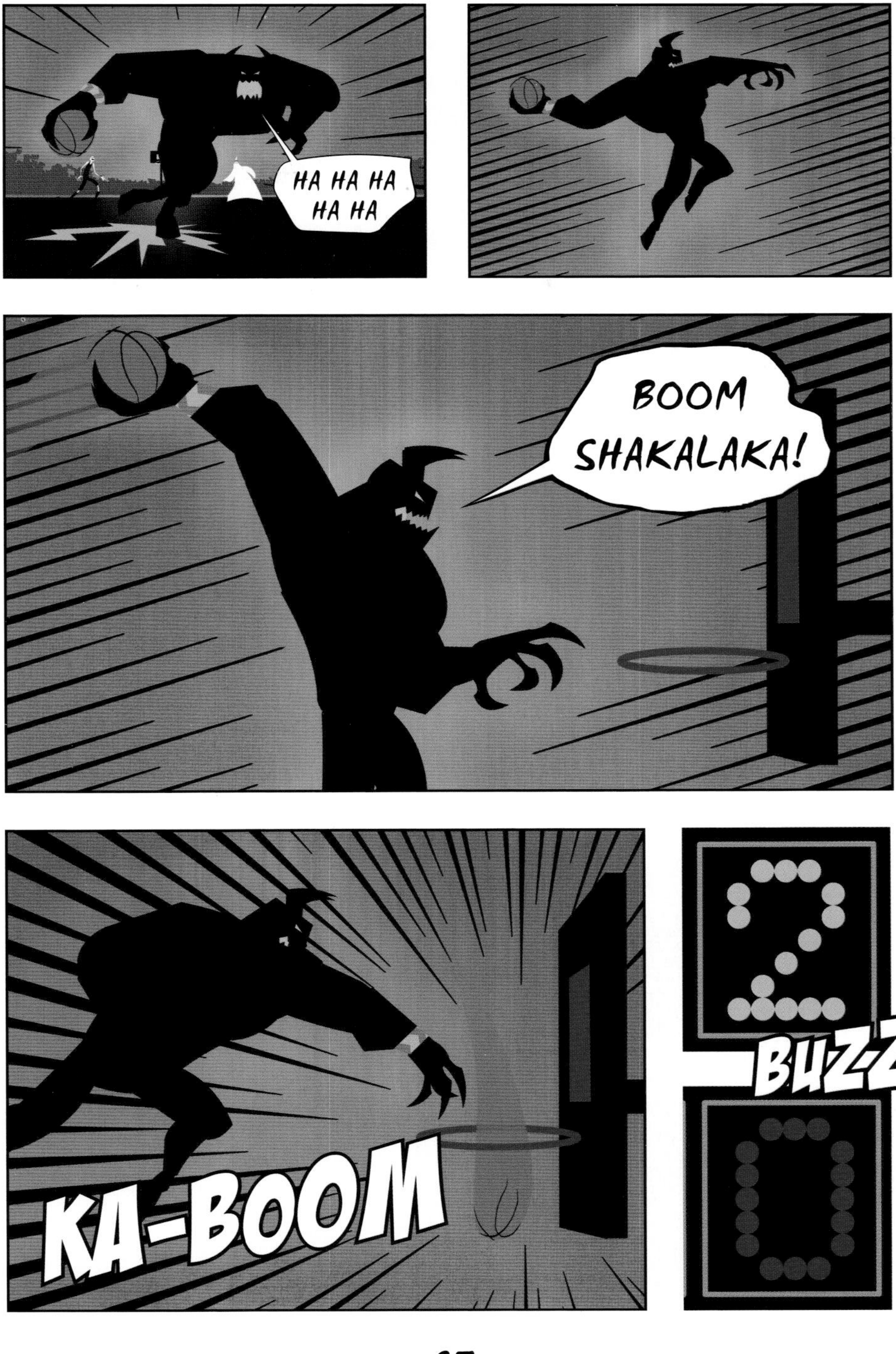
HA HA HA
HA HA
BOOM
SHAKALAKA!
KA-BOOM
BUZZ

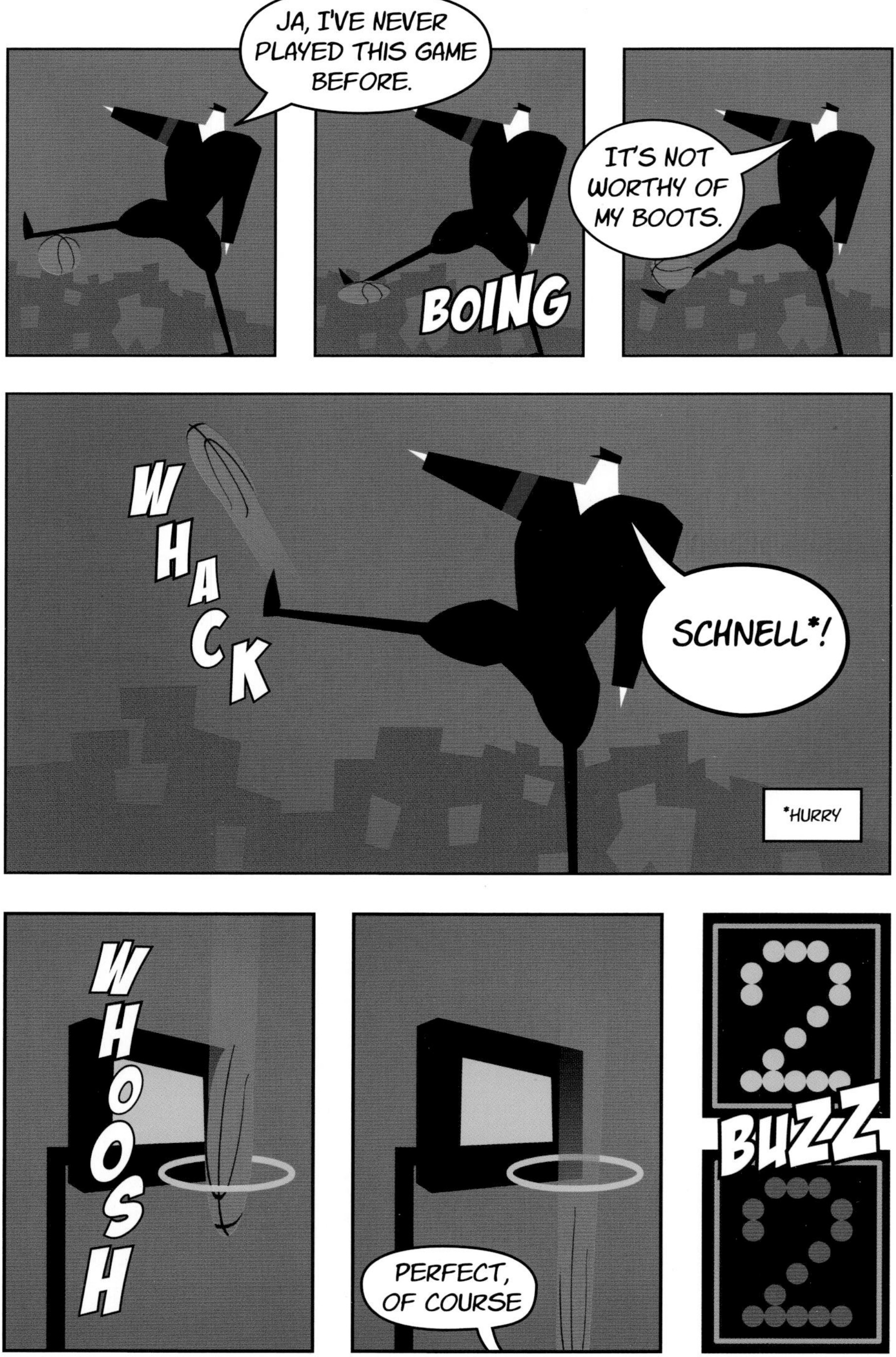
JA, I'VE NEVER PLAYED THIS GAME BEFORE.
BOING
IT'S NOT WORTHY OF MY BOOTS.
WHACK
SCHNELL*!
*HURRY
WHOOSH
PERFECT, OF COURSE
2
BUZZ
2

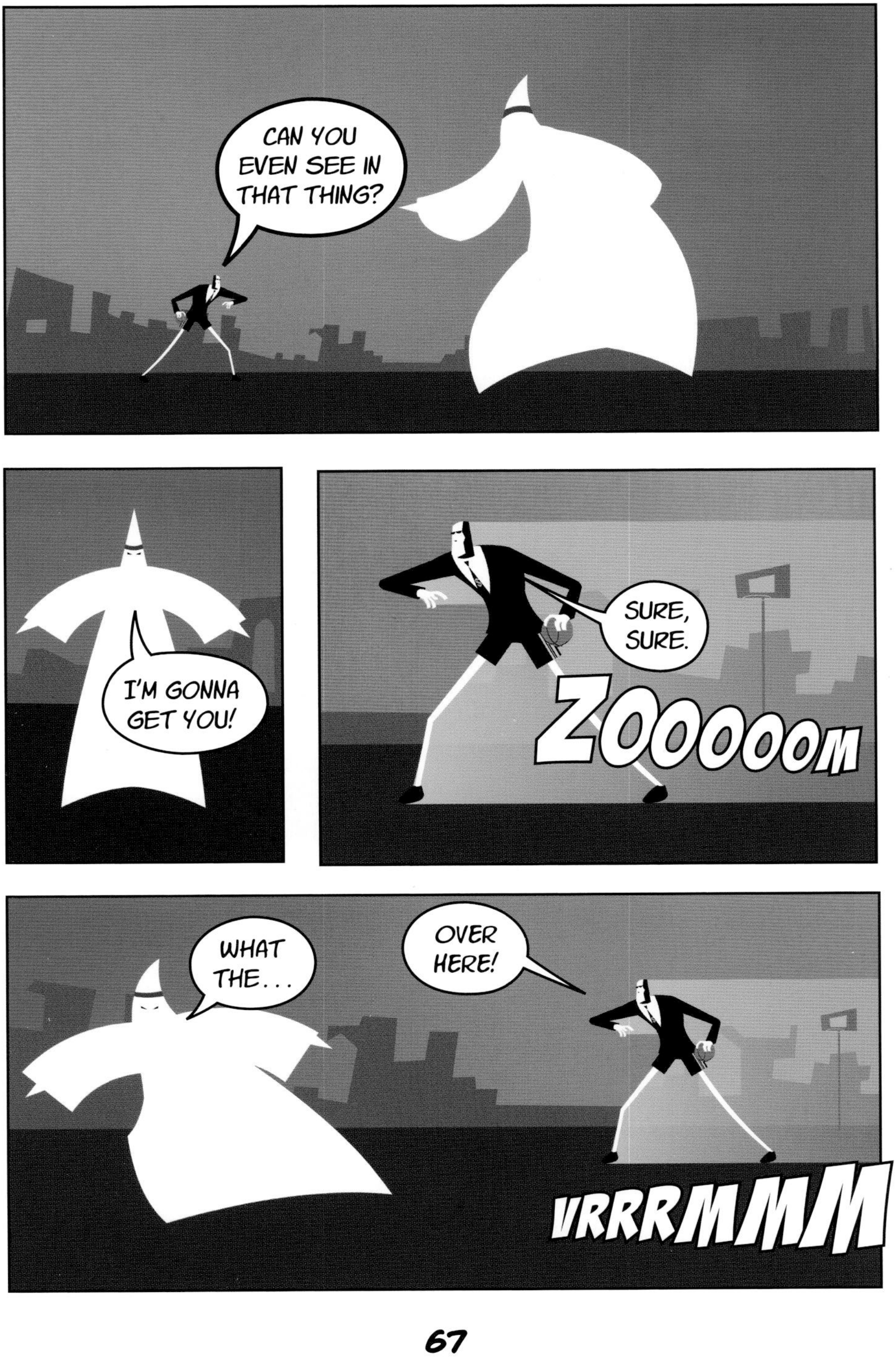
CAN YOU EVEN SEE IN THAT THING?
I'M GONNA GET YOU!
SURE, SURE.
ZOOOOOM
WHAT THE. . .
OVER HERE!
VRRRMMMM

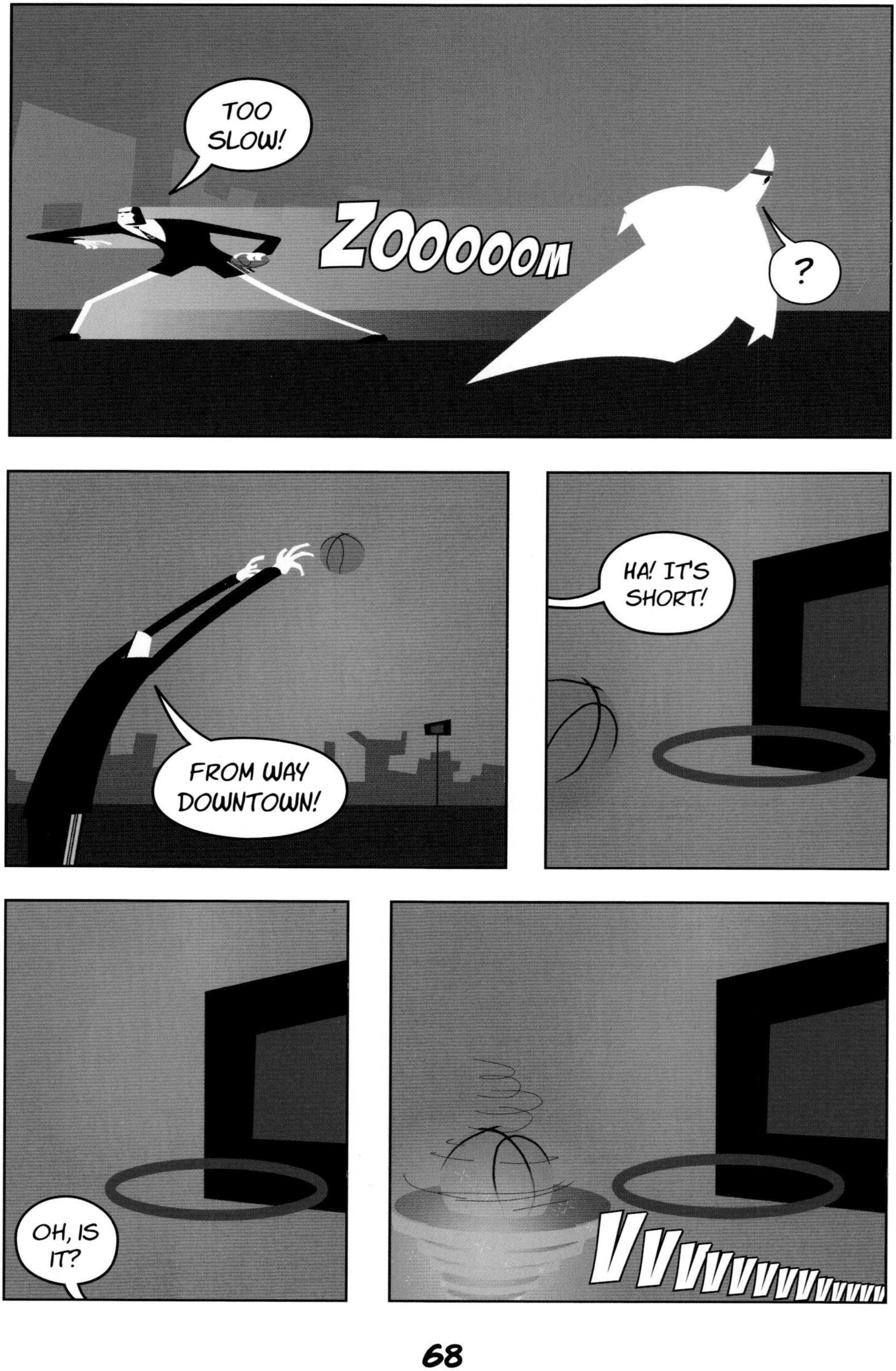
TOO SLOW!
ZOOOOOOM
?
FROM WAY DOWNTOWN!
HA! IT'S SHORT!
OH, IS IT?
VVVVVVVVVVVVVVVV

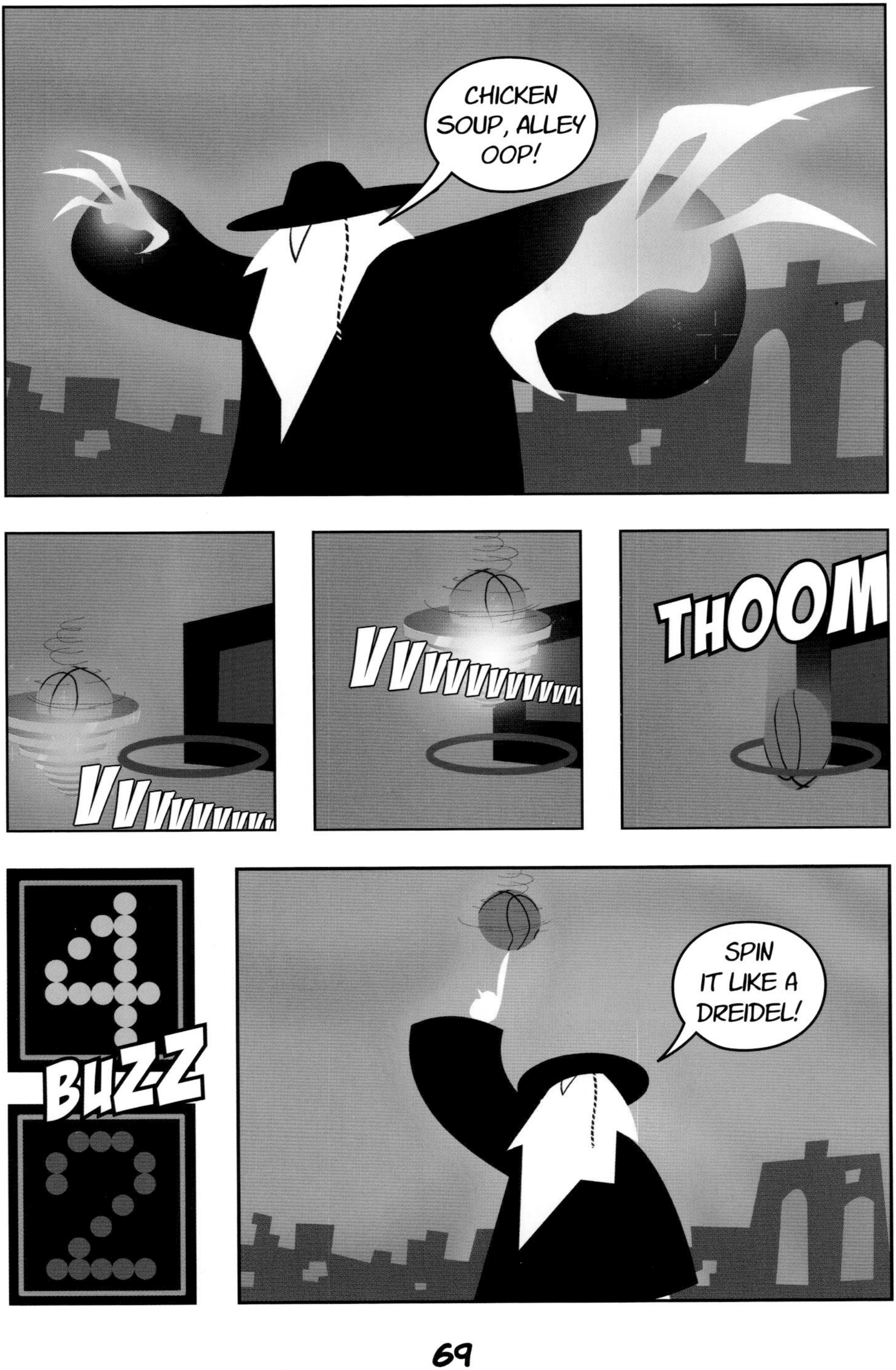
CHICKEN SOUP, ALLEY OOP!
VVVVVVVVVVV
VVVVVVVVVVVVVV
THOOM
BUZZ
SPIN IT LIKE A DREIDEL!

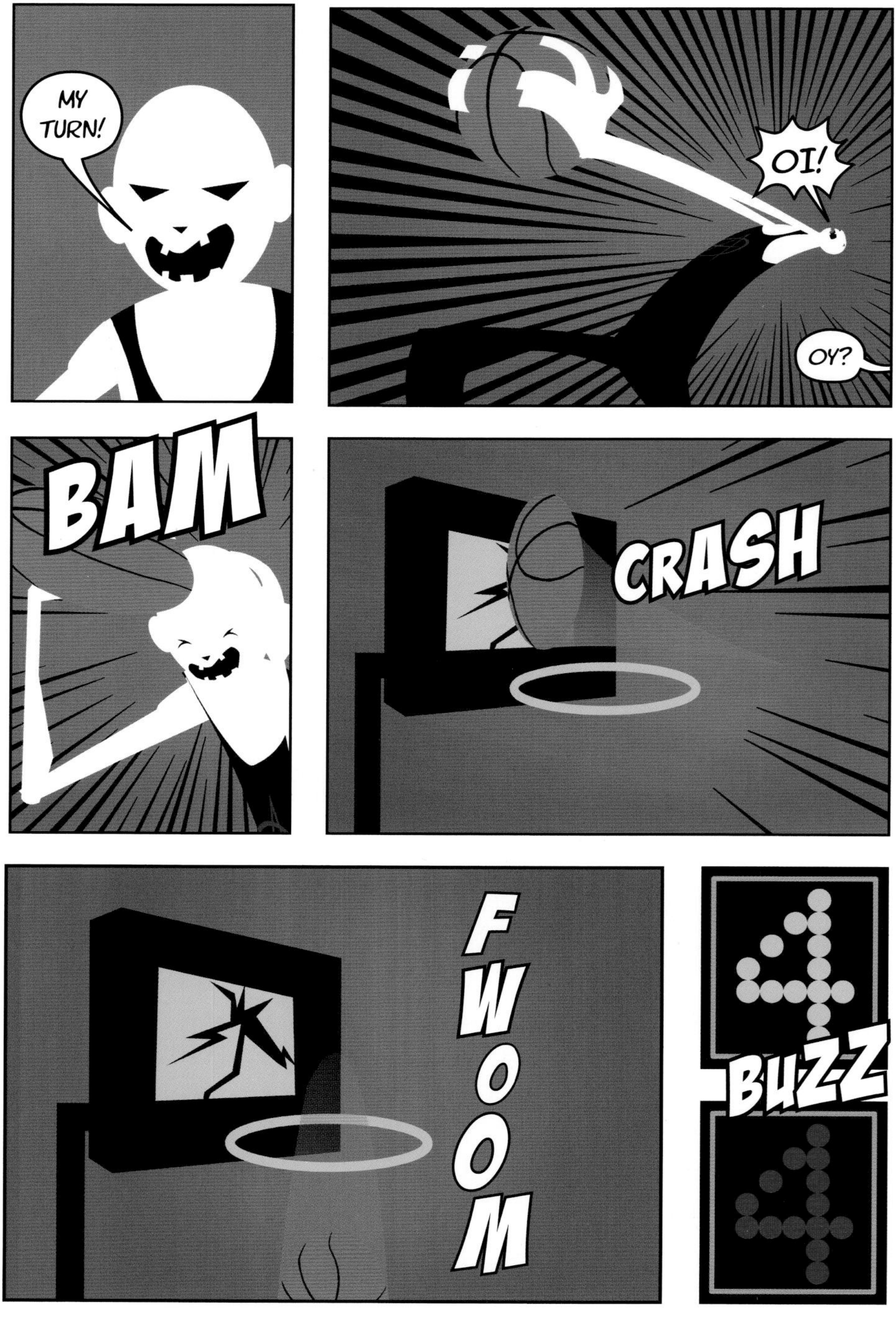
MY TURN!
OI!
OY?
BAM
CRASH
FWOOM
BUZZ

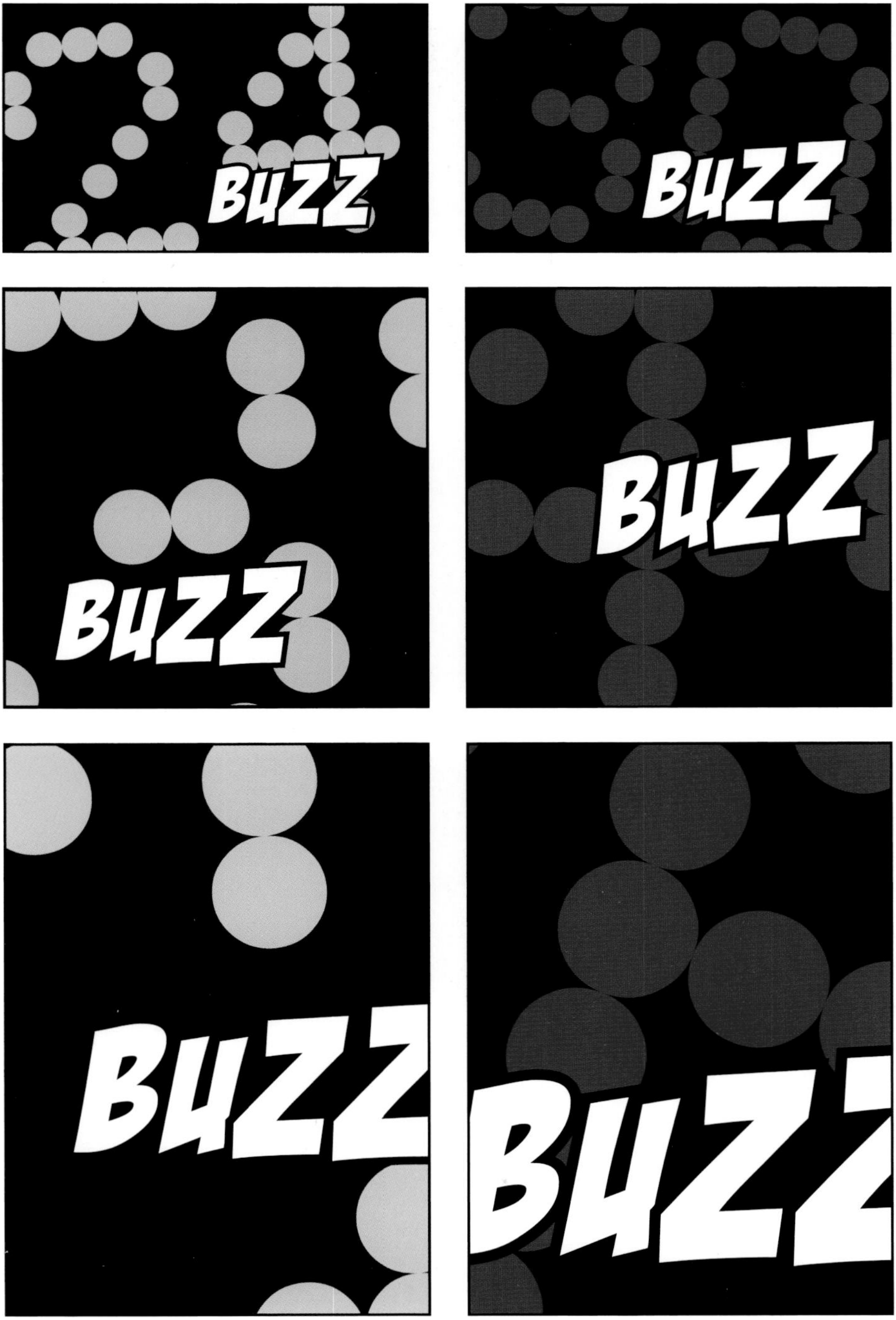
BuZZ
BuZZ
BuZZ
BuZZ
BuZZ
BuZZ

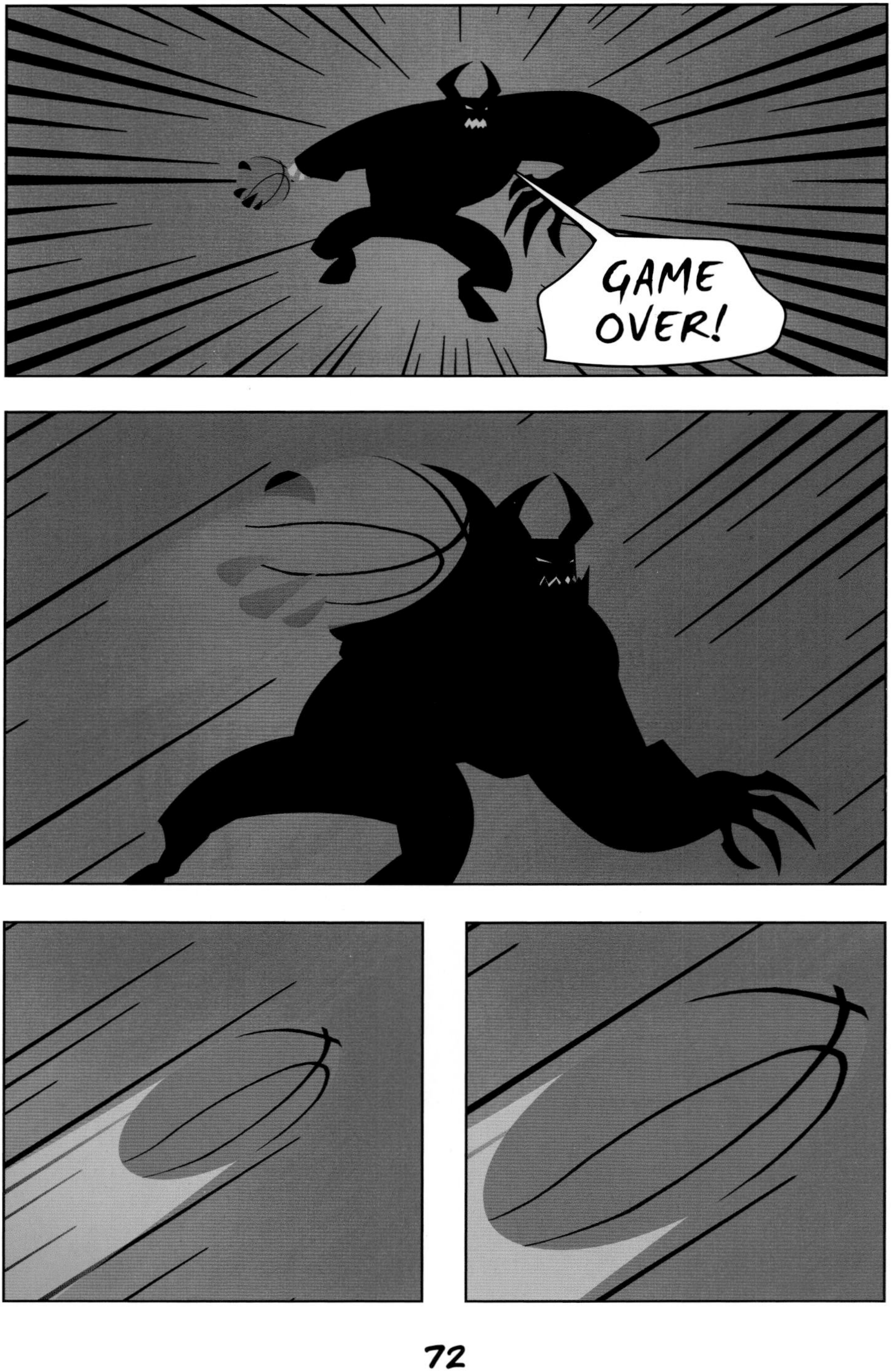
GAME OVER!

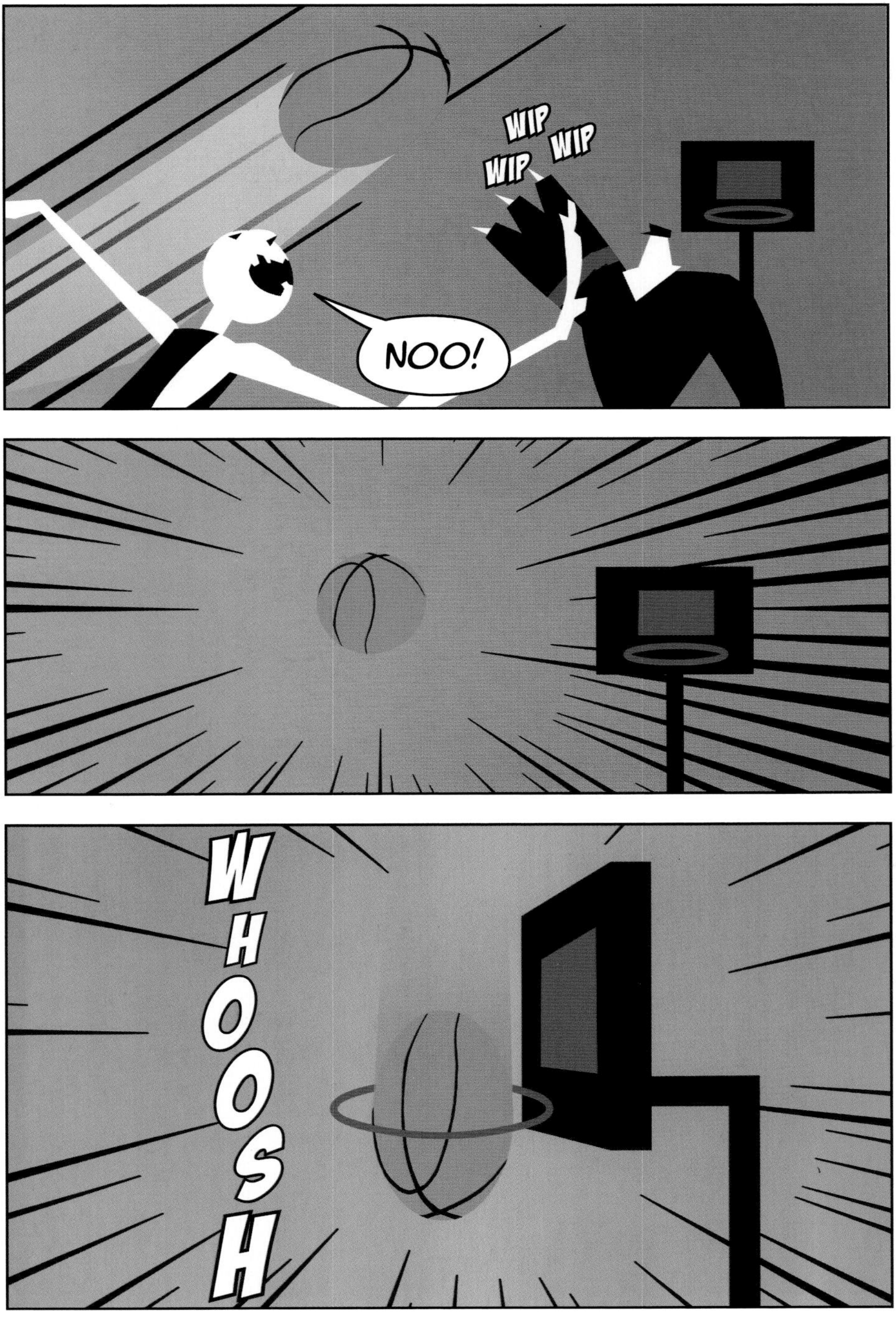
WIP
WIP
WIP
NOO!
WHOOSH

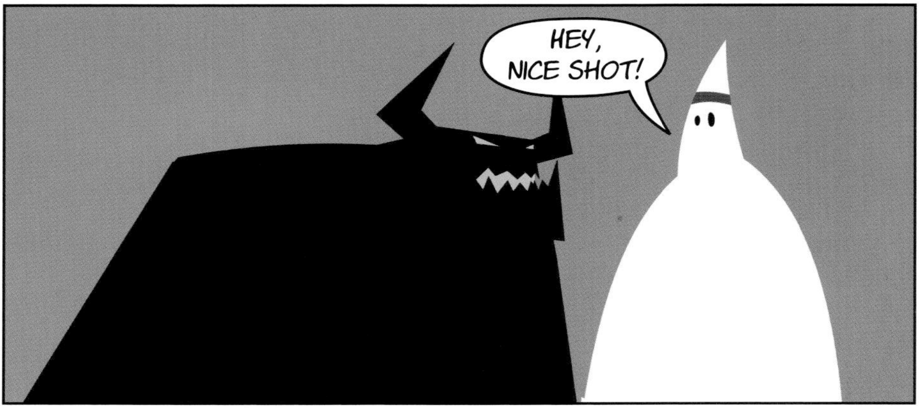
HEY,
NICE SHOT!

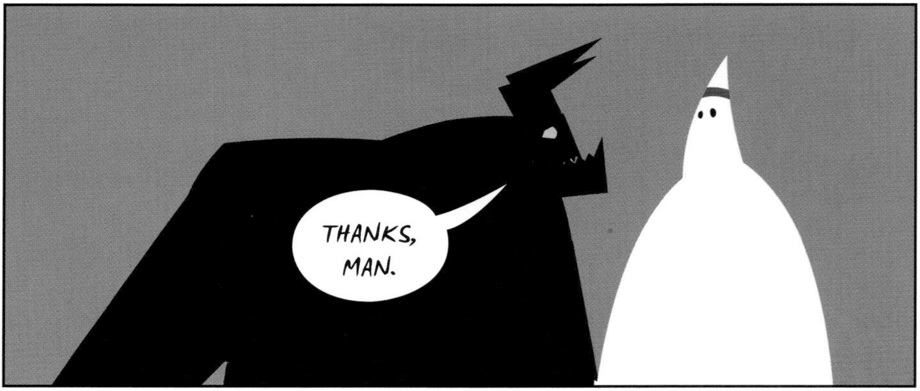
THANKS,
MAN.

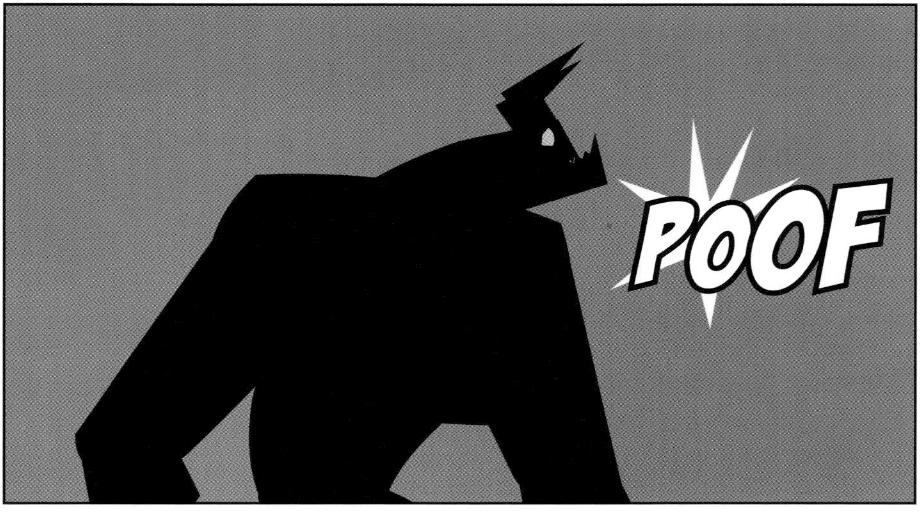
POOF

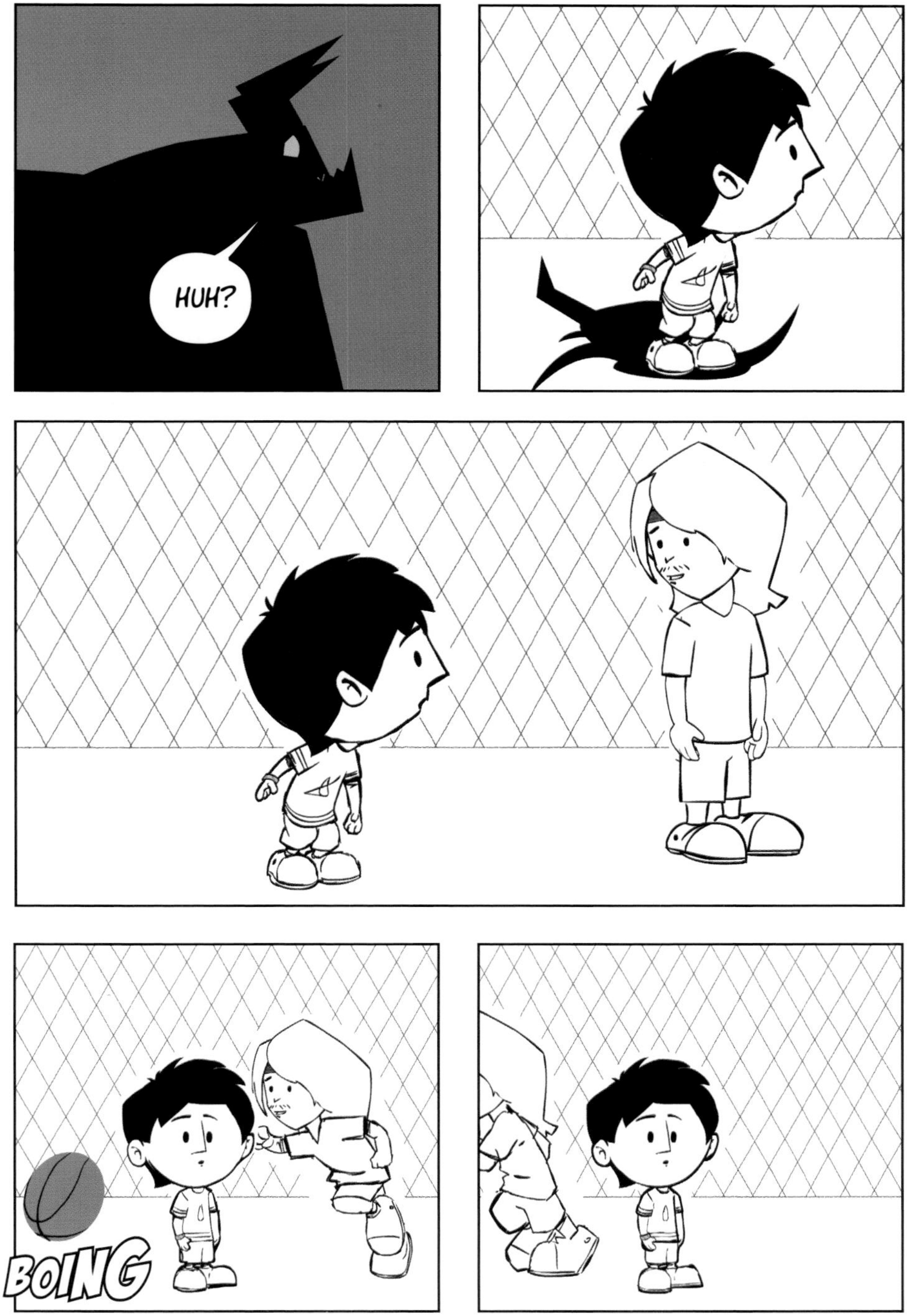
HUH?
BOING

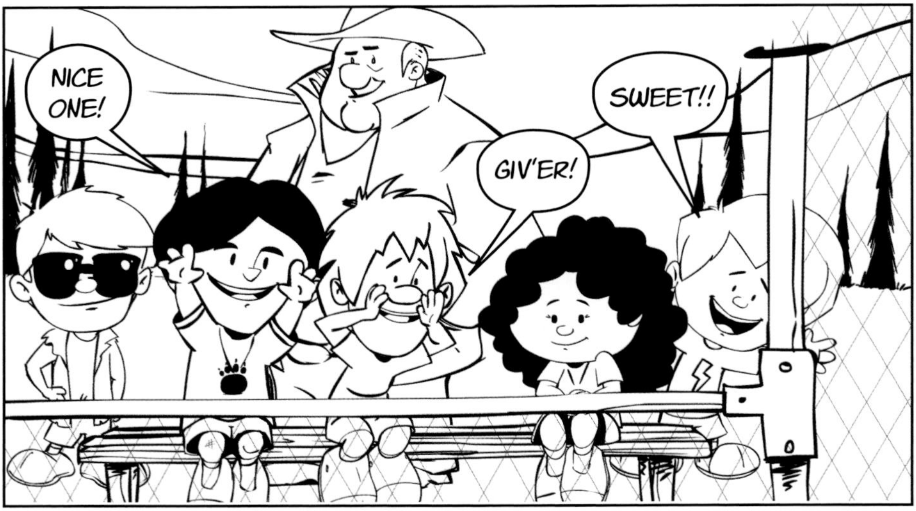
NICE ONE!
GIV'ER!
SWEET!!
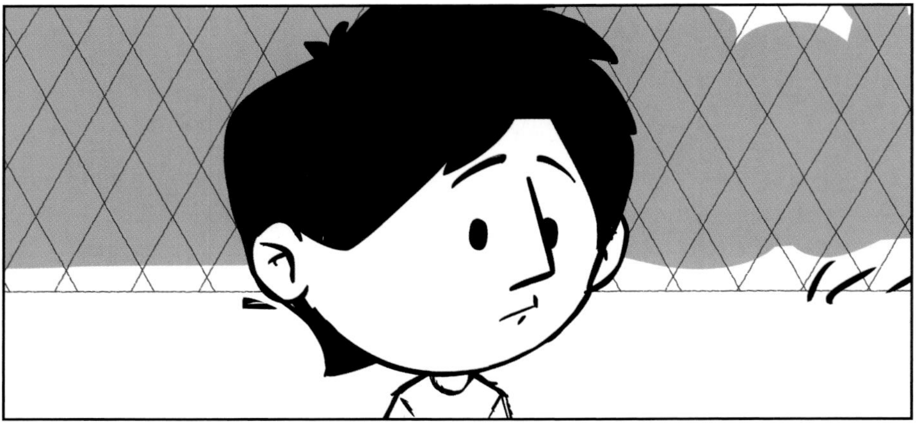
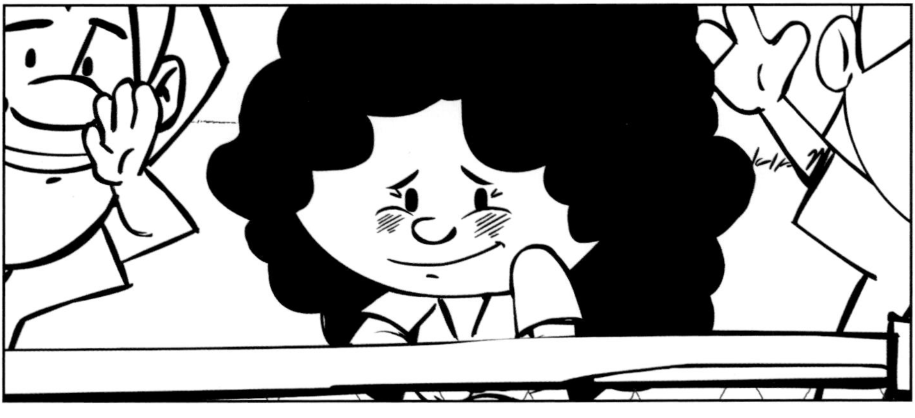

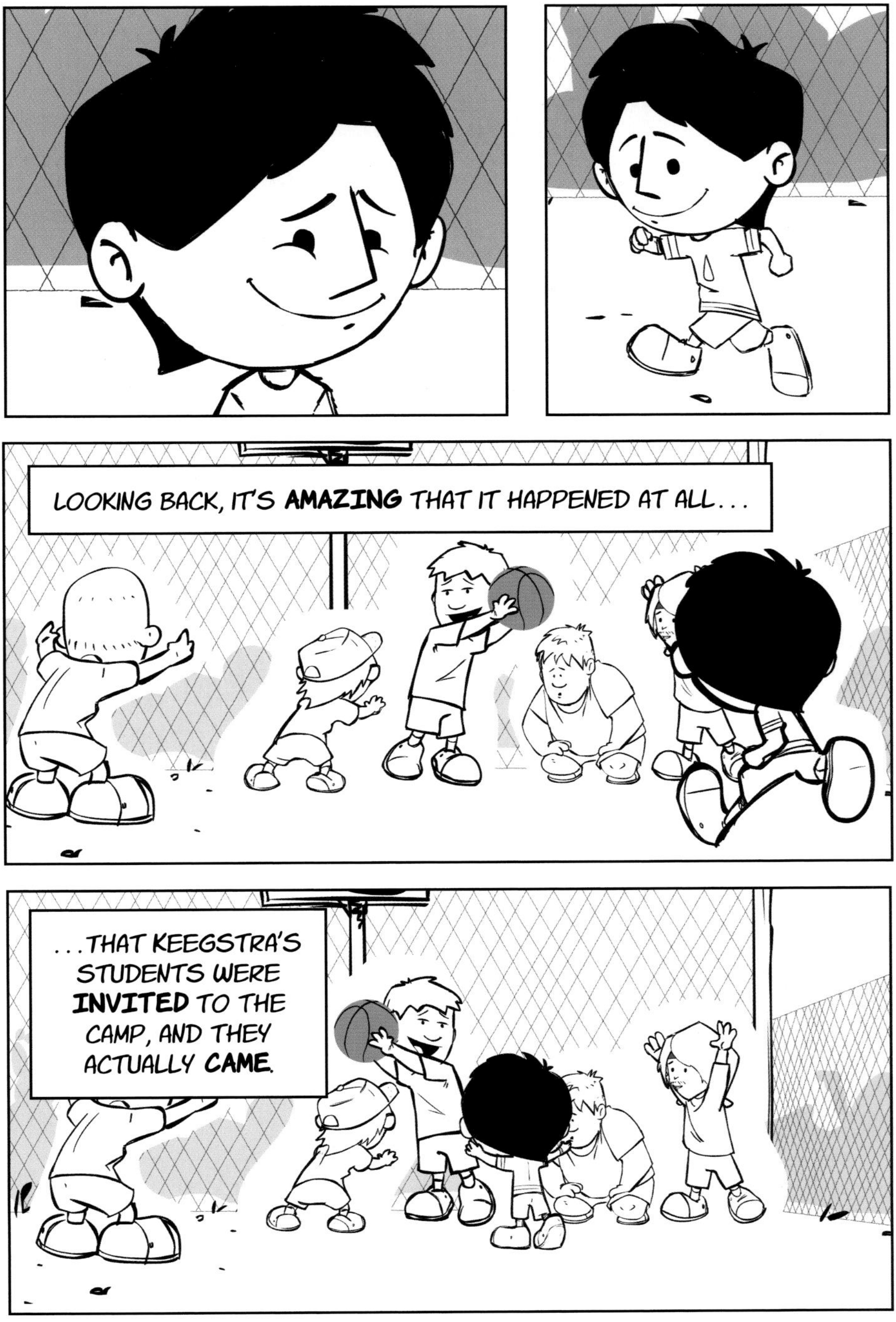
LOOKING BACK, IT'S **AMAZING** THAT IT HAPPENED AT ALL...
...THAT KEEGSTRA'S STUDENTS WERE **INVITED** TO THE CAMP, AND THEY ACTUALLY **CAME**.

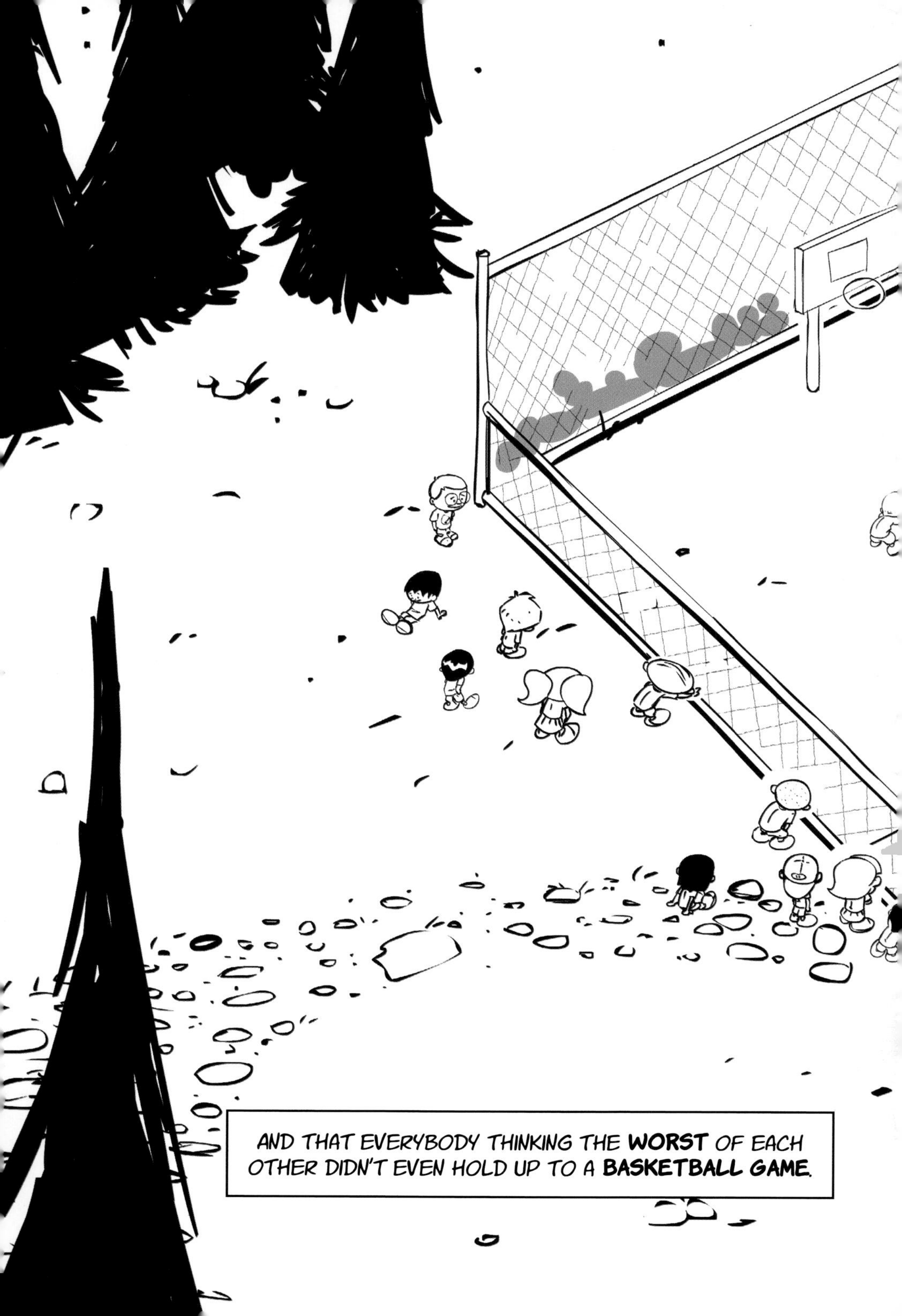
AND THAT EVERYBODY THINKING THE **WORST** OF EACH OTHER DIDN'T EVEN HOLD UP TO A **BASKETBALL GAME**.

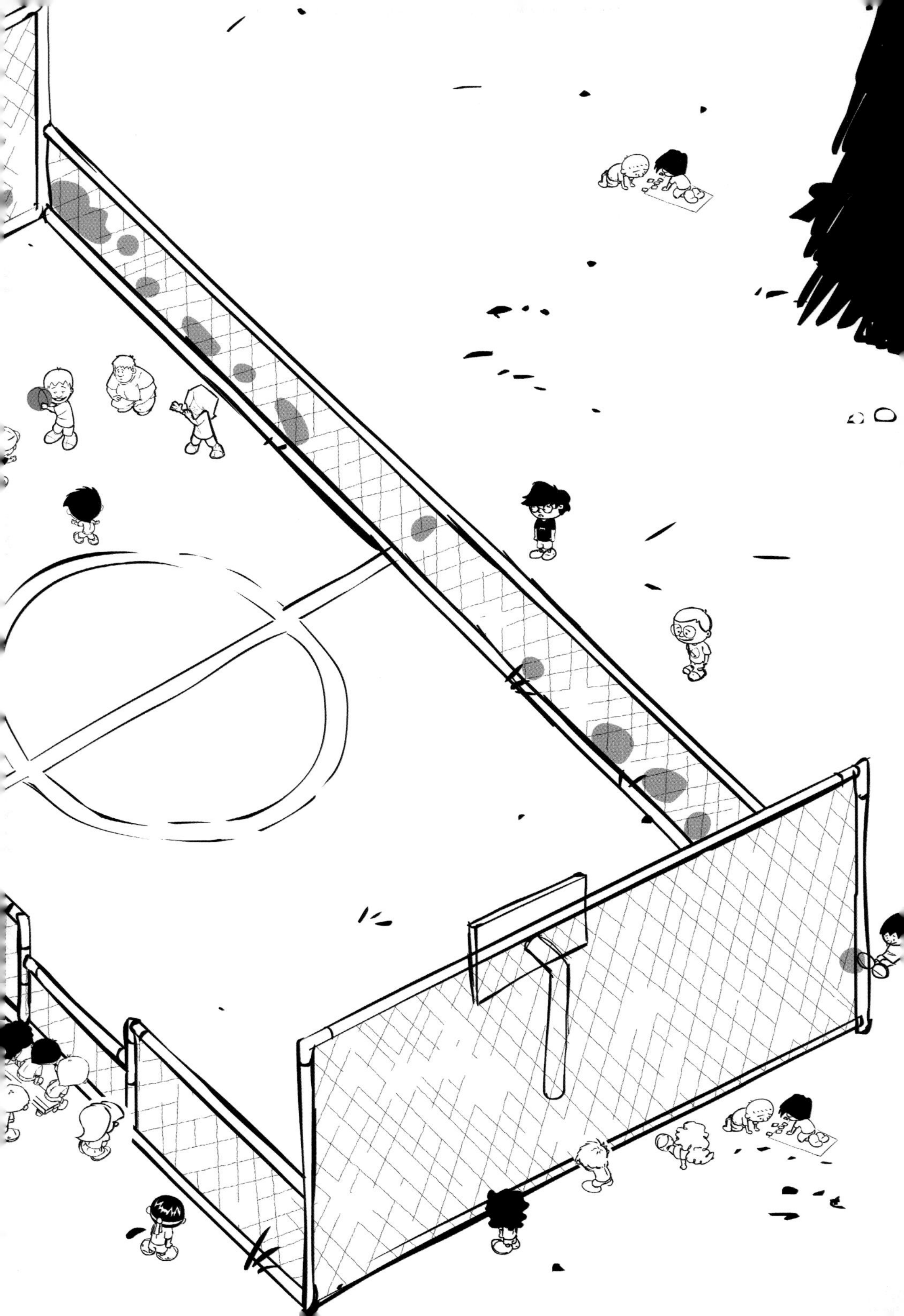

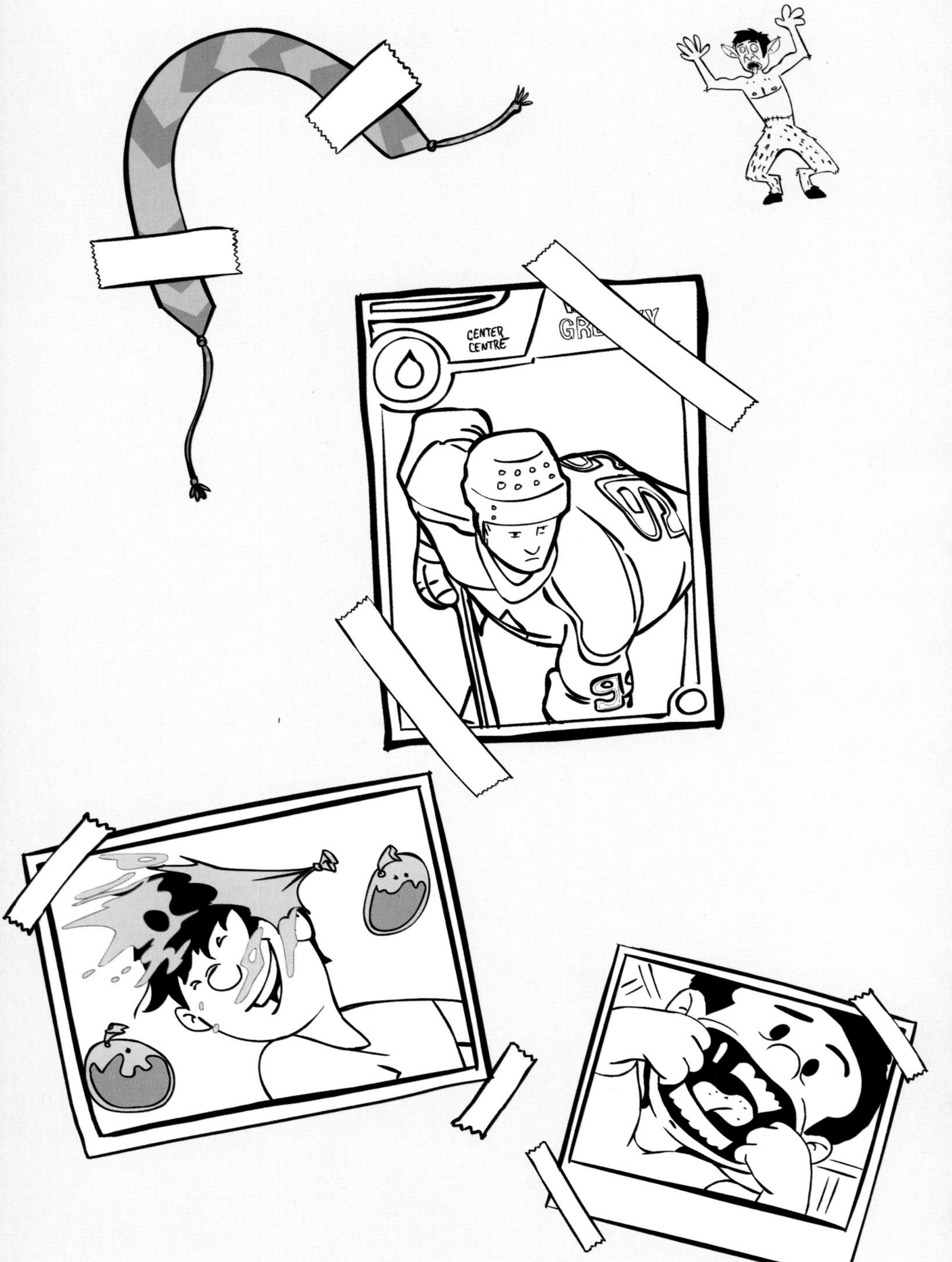
CENTER
CENTRE

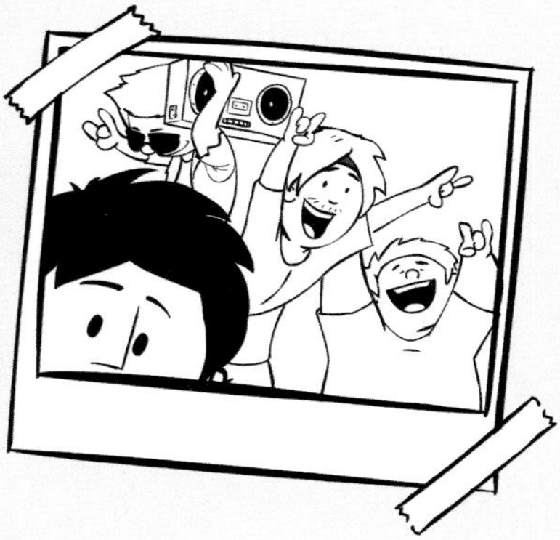

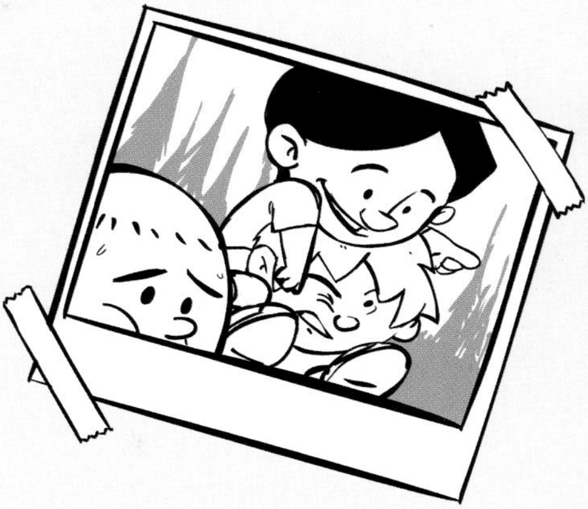

Eckville students can attend Jewish camp at Pine Lake

By JACK WILSON
of The Advocate

Eckville students will get a chance to enroll in a Jewish summer camp to counteract lessons taught by former teacher Jim Keegstra.

Ed Olson, principal of Eckville Junior-Senior high school said today his students will be allowed to visit the B'nai B'rith camp at Pine Lake "hopefully in early July."

Mr. Keegstra was fired from the school in December for teaching anti-Semitic material.

Attendance at the camp will be voluntary. A preliminary survey shows about 10 per cent of the school's 186 students would be willing to attend, he said.

"It's open to any student.

"We'll be sending letters home with the students so they can work it out with their parents."

Mr. Olson met members of the Jewish community in Edmonton this week. He declined discussing how the camp will be run or what events will take place.

"I think that is something that can be better looked at following the camp," he said.

"We both agreed to try and play down the publicity. We felt it would be better not to publicize it so much for the sake of the students," Mr. Olson said.

Pine Lake is 40 km southeast of Red Deer.

Jack Wilson. "Eckville students can attend Jewish camp at Pine Lake." *Red Deer Advocate*, May 20, 1983.

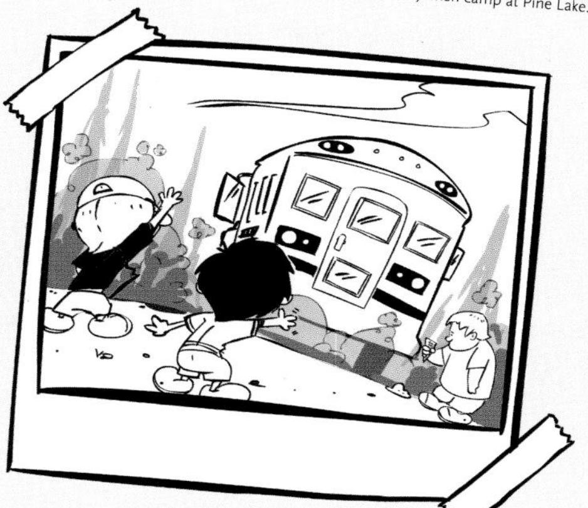

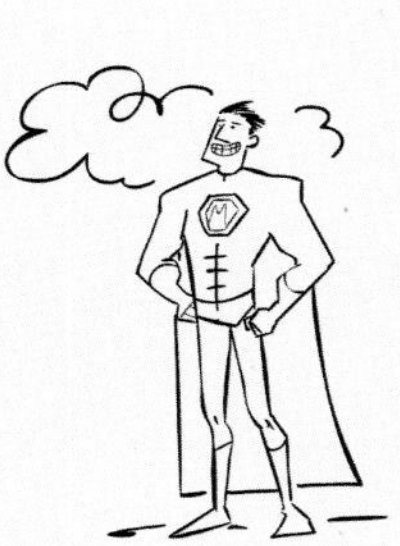

GOING TO THE KEEGSTRA TRIAL

After losing his job as mayor of Eckville and having his teaching certificate canceled by the Minister of Education, in 1985 Jim Keegstra finally stood trial for criminally promoting hatred against Jewish people. The trial took place in Red Deer, Alberta.

Twenty-three of Keegstra's former students testified. The Crown prosecutors argued that his ex-student's notes and essays proved that Keegstra was inciting hate. Keegstra never denied that he taught anti-Semitic material. His lawyer instead argued that the anti-hate law is a violation of Keegstra's right to free speech. Since the anti-hate law stated that no accused could be found guilty if they could prove that their statements of hatred were true, Keegstra testified for 26 days as his lawyer tried to prove his client's anti-Semitic conspiracy theories in court. Coverage of the trial in the local papers led to some sensational and problematic headlines:

Jews spread Holocaust 'hoax'—trial

Richard Helm. "Jews spread Holocaust 'hoax' — trial." *Edmonton Journal*, May 2, 1985

Jews planned
to rule world,
pupil testifies

Judy Monchuk. "Jews planned to rule world, pupil testifies."
Red Deer Advocate, April 15, 1985.

Keegstra's trial was an awful thing to witness, but many people from Jewish communities in Edmonton, Calgary and across Canada decided it was important to experience the trial for themselves and stand up to all the lies. At my Jewish elementary school in Edmonton, my Grade 6 class had been learning about the Holocaust. Our teacher — who was furious over the daily news coverage about this man who was spreading conspiracy theories and denying that the Holocaust had even happened — decided to take us to the trial.

That day we weren't just a busload of Jewish kids on a field trip to Red Deer, we were a symbol — of Jewish perseverance, of strength. Like the other Jewish people from across the province and country who had come to witness the trial, we demanded, "How dare you say such terrible things about us to our faces?"

Personally, I was absolutely terrified at the thought of Keegstra even looking at me. I was also creeped out to hear his voice in person after all the 6 o'clock news stories I'd watched with my family. What craziness would he be talking about today? Would we be on the news? Was this officially the worst field trip of all time?

But after we arrived, we found out that we couldn't attend that day. We headed back to Edmonton on highway 2 without ever having stepped inside the courtroom.

As the weeks went on, the spotlight on Keegstra's racist views and actions revealed the truth: his "lessons" were nothing but hateful, easily disprovable lies.

His trial ended after 70 days — making it at that point the longest jury trial in Alberta history. Keegstra was convicted and fined $5,000, which he tried to appeal. Keegstra's appeals went all the way to the Supreme Court of Canada, which eventually decided in 1996 that the crime of promoting hatred is a reasonable limit on the right of freedom of expression.

Keegstra was successfully convicted of criminally promoting hatred of Jewish people, which was an important test of Canada's hate speech legislation. It forced Canadians to have an uncomfortable public debate about racism in our society, and it reminded everyone about the importance of thinking critically and — like Susan Maddox — we all have a personal responsibility to stand up to hate.

DISCUSSION QUESTIONS

How do the main character's own feelings of worry (homesickness) influence his feelings of the visiting campers? How do our own feelings influence how we think about events around us?

Describe the feelings and thoughts of the campers when they find out that the Eckville students are coming to the Jewish camp to play basketball.

What are some similarities between how each group of kids feels about the other group? How do each of these perspectives contribute to racism?

Why does the author transform the characters during the basketball game? What is he trying to demonstrate by doing this? Does the author or the main character show any biases in these transformations? Does one team stand out more than the other? In what ways?

How different is the second half of the game? How differently are the characters interacting? What causes this sudden change?

What ultimately dissolves the tension between the two basketball players? Do you believe that it is that easy to dissolve tension?

What are some ways that kindness and empathy are depicted in the story? Think of or share your own memory of a simple act of kindness or empathy that has had a big impact on your life.

What other title could this story have?

What makes this a story about Holocaust denial? What do you know about Holocaust denial? Why do you think some people put so much effort into denying the Holocaust?

How does Holocaust denial impact the characters in this story? Discuss how you think it impacts the Jewish campers and the non-Jewish kids?

Why is it important that we remember and talk about the Holocaust?

Questions written by Benje Bondar and Anna-Mae Wiesenthal

GLOSSARY

ANTI-SEMITISM: Hostility toward or discrimination against Jewish people based on their religious, ethnic, racial or cultural identity.

CONSPIRACY THEORY: A theory that certain events or circumstances are the result of a secret plot by powerful individuals or groups.

GENOCIDE: The deliberate and systematic destruction of a group of people because of their ethnicity, nationality, religion or race.

THE HOLOCAUST: The systematic, state-sponsored genocide of more than six million European Jews as well as members of other persecuted groups by Nazi Germany and its allies during World War II.

HOLOCAUST DENIAL: An anti-Semitic conspiracy theory that asserts that the Holocaust did not happen or was greatly exaggerated.

KU KLUX KLAN (KKK): An American post-Civil War society advocating white supremacy historically through violence and terrorism.

LEGISLATURE: An elected assembly with the authority to make laws for a political entity, such as a country, province or city.

NAZI: A member of the German fascist political party controlling Germany from 1933 to 1945 under Adolf Hitler. Also, anyone who adopts the beliefs and policies of the Nazis.

PREJUDICE: Dislike of or unfair treatment toward a person or a group of people because of their race, religion, gender, identity or appearance. This attitude is often irrational or ill-informed.

PREMIER: The elected head of government of one of Canada's provinces or territories.

RACIST: A person who is prejudiced against or antagonistic toward a particular racial or ethnic group, typically one that is a minority or marginalized. Also, someone who believes one race is inherently superior to another race.

SKINHEAD: Someone belonging to a youth gang whose members have close-shaven hair, are sometimes violent and often adopt white supremacist beliefs.

WHITE SUPREMACIST: A person who believes that white people are superior to all other races and should, therefore, dominate society.

ACKNOWLEDGMENTS

Thanks to the parents and community leaders of both the Edmonton Jewish community and the Eckville community who decided to work together to combat the lies and hatred Keegstra was spreading. This includes Susan Maddox, Margaret Andrew, Ed Olsen, Herb Katz, Hillel Boroditsky, Lew Hamburger, Bill Meloff and everyone who made the day of "fun and fellowship" happen back in 1983.

Thanks to David Bercuson and Douglas Wertheimer for their book *A Trust Betrayed: The Keegstra Affair* (1985), which was an invaluable resource, and to the reporters and editors from the *Red Deer Advocate*, the *Edmonton Journal* and the *Calgary Herald* who covered the story.

Big thanks to Sean Covernton for bringing this story to life with so much sensitivity, humor and heart.

Thanks to the National Film Board of Canada's Pacific and Yukon Centre and everyone who was involved with the 2011 film *The Basketball Game*: Yves J. Ma, Adam Damelin, Tracey Friesen, Selwyn Jacob, Teri Snelgrove, Jennifer Roworth, Wes Machnikowski, Kathryn Lynch, Martin Rose, Jill Sharpe, Svend-Erik Eriksen, Ann Marie Fleming, Saphren Ma, Janine Steele, Elisa Chee, Greg Masuda, Kelly Fox, Julie Arseneault, Peter Eliuk, Bill Sheppard and all the Cooking Creative workshop participants.

Thanks to everyone who I couldn't have made the film without: Galit Mastai, Earle Snider, Ruth Snider, Adam Snider, Lauren Sky, Rivvy Meloff, Danny Freedman, Barry Cooper, Heather Puttock, Jeff Topham, Moshe Mastai, Renee MacCarthy, Michael Scholar Jr. and Kailey Carruthers.

Thanks to everyone who worked on the graphic novel adaptation: Galit Mastai, Julie Takasaki, Steve Cameron, Mary Graziano, Shirley Vercruysse, Lionel Koffler, Sam Tse, Hartley Millson, Martha Rans and Daniel Oh. And thanks to everyone who helped out, including Earle Snider, Tslila Barzel, Mike Silverman, Howie Silverman, Claudia Ho Lem, Nadina Kaminer, Dani Elias, Benje Bondar, Anna-Mae Wiesenthal, Stacy Shaikin, Jared Shore, Byron Hackett of the *Red Deer Advocate* and the Jewish Archives and Historical Society of Edmonton and Northern Alberta.

And special thanks to Wolfie, my dog, who was by my side the entire time — what a good boy!

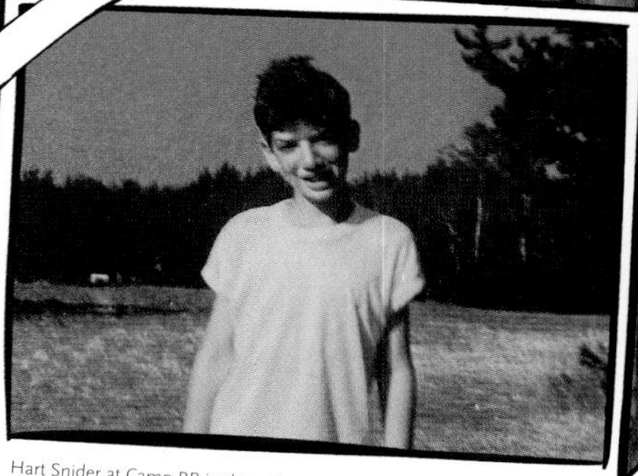

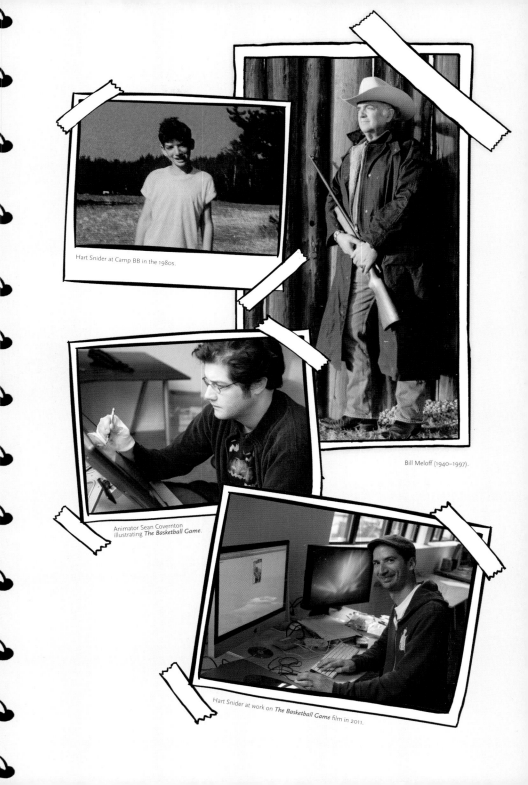

Hart Snider at Camp BB in the 1980s.

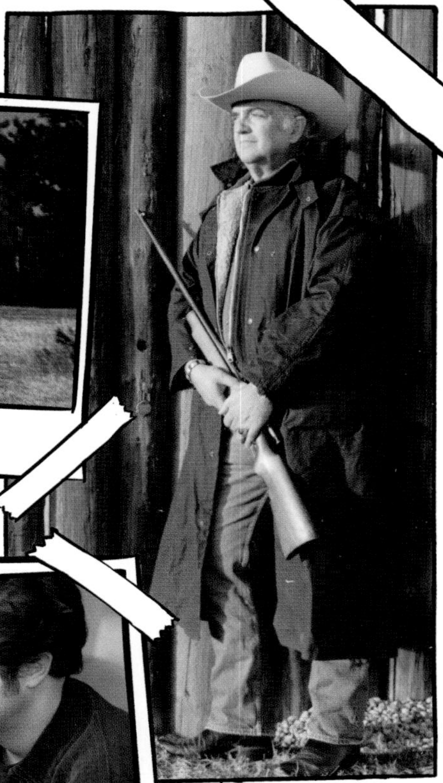

Bill Meloff (1940–1997).

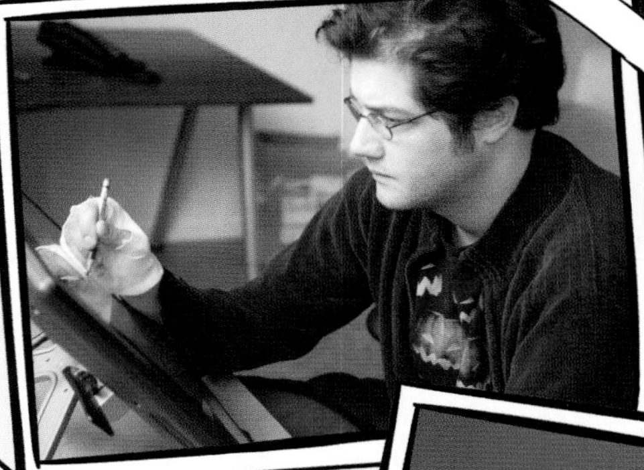

Animator Sean Covernton illustrating *The Basketball Game*.

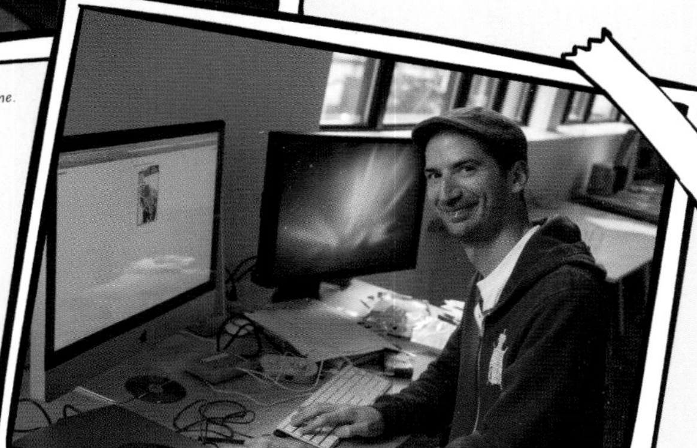

Hart Snider at work on *The Basketball Game* film in 2011.

Hart Snider is a writer and filmmaker living in Vancouver, British Columbia. He loves hanging out with his family, editing documentaries, reading comics and graphic novels, cheering for the Edmonton Oilers and staying up late. His animated films *The Basketball Game* and *Shop Class* are streaming worldwide on NFB.ca and the National Film Board of Canada (NFB) app.

Sean Covernton was born in Winnipeg, Manitoba, and moved to Vancouver, British Columbia, to pursue his dreams of making cartoons for a living, which he happily does to this very day.

The story was written and drawn in Vancouver, British Columbia, on the traditional, ancestral and unceded territory of the Coast Salish peoples: Sḵwx̱wú7mesh (Squamish), Stó:lō and Səl̓ílwətaʔ/Selilwitulh (Tsleil-Waututh) and xwməθkwəy̓əm (Musqueam) Nations.